BREADS OF THE SOUTHWEST

BREADS OF THE SOUTHWEST

Recipes in the Native American, Spanish, and Mexican Traditions

BETH HENSPERGER

PHOTOGRAPHY BY LAURIE SMITH

CHRONICLE BOOKS

SAN FRANCISCO

ACKNOWLEDGMENTS

Thanks goes to my literary agent extraordinaire, Martha Casselman, who believes in my projects and who is a constant source of encouragement. Special appreciation goes to the production and design staff at Chronicle Books for making my books look so good and adding their creative talents; to Susan Derecskey, who keeps me clear, accurate, and organized; and of course to Bill LeBlond, Leslie Jonath, and Sarah Putnam, the editors who carefully guided this project.

I am delighted to have had the opportunity to talk with the following people who generously shared anecdotes, information on ingredients and nomenclature, colorful stories, traditional and inventive recipe suggestions throughout my research: the people at Ancient City Press; Elaine Corn; Susan Curtis of the Santa Fe School of Cooking; Janet Fletcher; the folks at the Hopi Cultural Center on Second Mesa; the Laguna Pueblo Tribal Office and Library staff; Adrian Leyva, Jill Mellick and Barbara Guth of the University of New Mexico Press; Southwest chef and foodways expert Joyce Piotrowski; Pamela Polivka of Frieda's, Inc.; the people at the Pueblo Cultural Center in Albuquerque; Cynthia Robbins of Tuba City; Mary Jo Turek for keeping my Spanish correct; Victoria Wise; Lionel Hernandez, who filled my ear with many a tale that spilled over into the spirit that created this work; and to my friend of unsurpassed generosity and accomplishment, who loves the food of the Southwest and provided me with the "famous tortilla griddle," Jacqueline Higuera McMahan.

Heartfelt thanks to the many recipe testers and former students, whose efforts and feedback are invaluable in a work of this scope: Judy Adam, Judith Armenta, Lori Atone, Sallie Doeg, Teresa Gubbin, Susan Guest, Phyllis Hensperger, Amanda Hesser, Jacquie McMahan, Marie Meseroll, Berit Meyer of Ramone's Bakery, Tracy B. Myers, Lou Pappas, Jennifer Quinton, Sharon Redgrave, and special appreciation to my friend Bobbe Torgerson.

Library of Congress Cataloging-in-Publication Data available.

ISBN 0-8118-0973-0

Printed in Hong Kong.

Designed by Gretchen Scoble

Distributed in Canada by Raincoast Books
8680 Cambie Street
Vancouver, British Columbia V6P 6M9

10 9 8 7 6 5 4 3 2 1

Chronicle Books
85 Second Street
San Francisco, California 94105

Web Site: www.chronbooks.com

CONTENTS

LAYERS

OF EARTH,

GRAIN, AND

FIRE

In this hidden nook, isolated from the outside world, people were contented to live their simple lives. Still holding to ceremonies carried on from the medieval age of faith and religious traditions . . . [T]he conical adobe ovens were seen smoking throughout the three villages, while the week's supply of bread and panocha was being baked. The mud ovens must be blessed before using them, or they won't bake the bread right; it will come out heavy and soggy. To bless the oven, a cross is laid on the floor of the oven, salt is sprinkled on the cross and prayers recited.

Cleofas M. Jaramillo, *Genuine New Mexico Tasty Recipes* (Ancient City Press, reprinted 1981)

The Southwest bread-making renaissance is more accurately described as a culinary evolution than revolution. The culture of the American Southwest is based upon the Indian corn civilization of Mexico and Central America which is thousands of years old. It was influenced by the ancient Mayan traditions, where the planting of a seed of corn was reason enough for a ceremony. Later part of New Spain after being claimed by the conquistadors, the area became colonized by missionaries, soldiers, ranchers, and orchardists, pioneer settlers and miners, sheepherders and wheat farmers living alongside the Native populations. This early development overlaps and affects the lives of the people of this century: both the avant-garde artist communities of the 1920s, and contemporary urbanization and industrialization.

Geographically covering an area including Arizona, southern Colorado, New Mexico, and Texas, the Southwest technically describes lands bordering on Old Mexico. It encompasses two deserts, the Sonoran and the Chihuahuan, and a vast cornucopia of ethnic culinary traditions that include Anglo and Hispanic traditions, as well as about seventy native cultures.

Age-old baking techniques are based extensively on those used by the local Native American Indians, especially the Pueblo tribes. Some sort of bread or gruel was the foundation for every meal. Today, the original ingredients and techniques are still the basis for a complex, aromatic array of breadstuffs, which are life-sustaining and soul-satisfying. Derived from a fragrant blend of Native, Spanish, and Anglo culinary traditions, the breads of the American Southwest are nothing short of sensational.

The story of a people's bread, a food they eat daily, is a good window on their history, their spiritual beliefs, their economy, and their agricultural practices. Because of corn's importance to the Natives of the Southwest, it became a central element of their culture and elaborate ceremonialism, especially for planting and harvest, to pay homage to the corn deities.

Bread inspires and accompanies local festivities. Myths surrounding corn, a grain native to the Americas, have been passed down through generations, and corn is the most important substance in rituals, as well as a daily breadstuff. Each pueblo has had its own name for corn (and every stage of its growth, from the first leaves, increments of stalk, ear and tassel formation), and calendars revolved around sowing times and harvest since the times of the now extinct agrarian Anasazi, predecessors of the Hopi, Zuni, and other Pueblo Indians. The Zuni describe cultivated stalks of corn as Mother Corn. Divinities personify every aspect of the corn plant and the life forces that create and guide its growth.

Some of the most characteristic and inventive Southwest breads have sprung from an almost-bare larder. Corn and wheat flour slap breads—tortillas, sopaipillas (the Indian popover or "sofa pillow"), and Indian fry bread— are the most popular. Puffy yeast hearth breads and quick skillet corn breads are also standard. Corn, also called maize, and such wild plants as amaranth, mesquite, *kwaakwi,* the wild wheatlike grass of the Hopi mesas, and acorns, were ground into coarse meals and flours for Native breads and flatbreads. These traditional breads made from wild plants and corn and, later, wheat, which came with the Spanish occupation, give us a link to age-old customs. These breads can be baked as effectively in modern gas or electric ovens as they were by old-fashioned methods.

Written recipes give form to baking, yet many native Southwest breads have only recently been committed to paper. In *Hopi Cookery* (University of Arizona Press, 1980), Jaunita Tiger Kavena records dozens of corn-based breads. These local bread recipes have remained virtually unchanged in form over generations, handed down orally within families.

Cornmeal treated with lime was ground by hand on a stone *metate,* a large sloping stone containing a shallow depression for the kernels, which were crushed with a *mano,* a small handheld oval stone resembling a rolling pin. It was women's work and hard labor, but the meal is now commercially processed and available in supermarkets both as *masa* dough and dried *masa harina.* Crusty smooth rounds of peasant-style bread still bake to the color of old adobe in centuries-old outdoor beehive ovens alongside flatbreads on hot stone griddles or sizzling-hot smooth black rocks. Breads are fried in hot fat in heavy cast-iron Dutch ovens or wrapped around a green piñon twig over open fires. Thin flaky stacks of blue-gray piki bread, a tradi-

tional Hopi flatbread often nicknamed Hopi cornflakes, have roots back thousands of years. Corn husk–wrapped steamed breads folded to form a half-moon shape have been made for centuries. Sourdough skillet and griddle ranch and camp breads are cooked over an open fire.

Today's Mexican-American bakeries abound with empanadas, cookies, pattern-top sweet rolls, and *bolillos,* the ever-popular crusty oval wheat roll. Favorite sweet yeast breads include pumpkin breads, sweet rolls such as *Pan Dulce* and *molletes, Pan de Muerto* for All Souls' Day, and *Rosca de los Reyes* for Twelfth Night. These breads are ever present at local celebrations, the myriad feasts in honor of the saints observed as fervently in the small clusters of pueblo village communities as in town.

Modern Southwest breads showcase a wide range of ingredients available throughout the United States; besides wheat and corn, grains like oats, buckwheat, quinoa, and wild rice; New England maple syrup; and imported tropical fruits. New recipes provide variations on indigenous ingredients, and in keeping with the old ways, flours ground from mesquite pods, sun-dried acorns, saguaro seeds, and amaranth are used today in combination with wheat and corn flour.

In researching the history of the locale and assembling a collection of recipes suitable for today's modern baker, I found a reworking of old recipes was just not enough. Bread as a staple food requires a direct presentation and recipes that are simple to visualize as well as to execute in a home kitchen. There are no intimidating techniques here; the recipes merge simple breadmaking basics with ingredients that have long been associated with the locale. At the heart of these Southwest breads is the cross-pollination of Native inventiveness with wild foods, Spanish Old World foods, and the Anglo-pioneer heritage. The combination of these elements personify a daily food that has adapted naturally from the layering of the past to the needs of people living today. Herein lies your own artful ability to express your creativity and respect for a food that is linked with faith and the wholeness of the earth.

NATIVE SUN: SIGHTS, SCENTS, AND INFLUENCES

Corn: The ear of corn (maize)
with all its seeds
represents the people and
all things in the universe.

An Illustrated Encyclopedia of Traditional Symbols
(Thames & Hudson, 1978)

The Navajo, literally "cultivated fields" in the Tewa language, live by the concept of *hozhó*, which is defined in the *Dictionary of the Navajo Language* as "beauty" and "harmony." A word with no exact English translation, the concept reflects a personal sense of inner harmony with the earth and sky. Every food, as well as the physical acts of growing, preparing, and eating it, has a spiritual dimension. Tools for food preparation—from woven wheat plaques for carrying and serving bread, to yucca sieves, to polished baking stones, to carved stirring sticks—are infused with a sense of the divinity of man's relationship to nature, a direct link to his immediate natural surroundings. Hogans, or Navajo dwellings, are constructed with forked posts that are blessed with corn pollen. Colored cornmeals and corn pollen are used ritually to bless sacred objects and participants, as well as in preparing sacred ceremonial breads.

For the Hopi and Zuni, an ear of corn wrapped in feathers and adorned with jewels was the symbol of a holy man. Women carried bread and corn cakes to the men in the kivas during sacred ceremonies. The Zuni have a story of a goddess who took a slab of lava to carve out the first grinding tools, the metate and mano, then showed the Zuni how to grind corn to a fine flour with them. The vast corn fields were dotted with elaborate scarecrows dressed in old clothes. Animal bones and scraps of fabric and fur were suspended from yucca twine, which crisscrossed the fields, to blow on the wind and scare off the crows. Sonoran Desert tribes portray the mesquite as the "tree of life," and the treelike saguaro cactus is regarded as having human attributes.

The Phoenix Salt River valley and part of the Gila River valley cover the remains of over a hundred miles of irrigation canals engineered by the early Hohokam agriculturalists. The summers are fiery hot and the winters bitterly cold. A description of a faraway land? Not at all; this is the American Southwest.

At first impression, the rugged high desert is an arid landscape, one that appears almost dead. Upon closer inspection, the sand with its shifting patterns, the baked earth, the massive guardian rocks burnt by the sun, and the azure sky revealed a land teeming with life: a tapestry of grasslands, chaparral piñon and ponderosa forests, and the subtle coloration of veined paloverde shrubs. Brown comes in an infinite number of appealing earth tones. The mesas, rock plateau tables with steep sides and flat tops, dormant volcanoes, petrified sand dunes, and deep-gorged canyons are bold and magnificent. Mountains that rise out of nowhere inspired many Navajo creation stories. Fire and earth meld boundaries between a sunset and baked earth. The interplay of earth, air, and fire gives a feeling of a land without limits.

A majority of the once populous Pueblo tribes have clustered in villages along the drainage basin of the upper Rio Grande for centuries, with the Zuni, Acoma, and Hopi firmly established on lonely high mesas to the west. Oraibi and Shungopovi on Hopi Mesa are the oldest continuously inhabited towns in the United States, with views of the three sacred San Francisco Peaks just north of Flagstaff, home of the kachinas. Mount Taylor, or the Turquoise Mountain, is the landmark for the southern entrance to Navajo land. Traveling north, the Navajo reservation dips into four states. Author Tony Hillerman calls this area the "Native American Holy Land."

The desert tribes of Tohono O'odham live in their ancestral lands of southern Arizona and the Sonoran desert, which they share with the Pima, descendants of the ancient Hohokam agriculturalists. Colorado River tribes farmed the fertile flood plains with subsistence crops of pumpkin, corn, and beans. The tribal name Mohave translates to "beside the water." The hunting and gathering Utes live dispersed within the northern Rio Grande pueblos and up into Colorado. Semi-nomadic bands of Pai tribes populate remote canyons, caves, river bottoms, and plateaus with tiny summer food gardens supplementing their gathering of wild foods. One of the branches of the Pai, the "blue-green water people" known as the Havasupai, live at the bottom of the Grand Canyon in the Shangri-la of the Southwest, Havasu Canyon.

Migrating prehistoric Native American hunters and gatherers have inhabited the Southwest for about forty thousand years. Early horticultural efforts emerged around 3000 B.C., with the radiocarbon analysis in Bat Cave, New Mexico, dating inch-long corn cobs at 3600 B.C. According to archaeologists, the indigenous peoples of the Southwest, mainly the Pueblos, have lived in agrarian communities for about two thousand years. They lived in one place, a pueblo, the vast single building that housed the entire settlement, although many moved to the cornfields during the summer months, and grew a remarkable amount of food through "flood farming" in the desert canyon clefts. In the warmer areas, around the lower Colorado River and southern Arizona, two crops of corn could be planted each year.

The nomadic Navajos and the people now called the Apache, came to settle in the Southwest, migrating from Canada nearly a thousand years ago. Their humble breads reflect the gathered desert wild plant foods of the past—mesquite pods, acorns, Arizona walnuts, saguaro, amaranth, and sunflower. The Pai and Navajos later adopted the corn-farming habits of the Pueblo peoples. The nonagricultural Apaches and other seminomadic desert tribes utilized dried wild plants, especially amaranth, or they planted small mountain cornfields in summer and moved to the lowlands in the winter.

In 1540, when Vasquez de Coronado made the first trek into the remote northern desert in search of the cities described by Cabeza De Vaca and his companions, primitive roving bands still traveled single file across a barren, unpeopled land while agriculturalists lived in multistoried stone and adobe towns where they stored rainwater and food, terraced planting areas, and practiced dry irrigation techniques dating back to the Anasazi. The first Spanish explorers visited Acoma and Zuni pueblos. The first permanent settlement was at San Juan Pueblo. In 1598, twenty-three years before the Pilgrims, the very first American Thanksgiving feast was celebrated on the banks of the Rio Grande by five hundred Spanish colonists and members of the Catholic order of Saint Francis led by Don Juan de Oñate with the Santo Domingo Pueblo Indians. The Zunis sprinkled sacred maize flour on the colonists, an honor reserved for the representatives of the gods. By the 1600s, treasure had been found, and silver mines in Chihuahua and Sonora attracted many laborers who settled there.

During the following two hundred years of Spanish colonization, settlers, Jesuits, and later Franciscan missionaries brought their own influences, which are now an integral part of the area: grapes, olives, citrus and fruit trees, sugar, rice, dairy products, and the enclosed adobe oven. The Mesilla Valley in southern New Mexico and El Paso became top wine-making areas, supplying the Catholic churches with sacramental wine. The trade routes along the Chihuahua Trail onto the *el camino real* from Mexico to Albuquerque, a land journey taking five to six months, brought country farmers to the area. The Territory of New Mexico, which included Arizona (Papago for the "place of little springs"), was born. Arizona's Sonoran Desert was sparsely settled. The Spanish chose to settle in pueblo villages, carving them into Spanish family land grants. This became a period of great unrest between the two cultures, with the Spanish creating a slave caste of the local people and a system of forced tribute.

The Spanish landed gentry planted more wheat than corn, as it thrived in the high valleys around Peñasco, on the border of Picuris Pueblo, and Taos, both in the Sangre de Cristo mountain range. Father Kino, a Franciscan priest, distributed wheat seeds to the local Pima and Pagagos in the early eighteenth century. Southern Arizona, near the Coahuíla and Nuevo León wheat-growing breadbasket of New Spain, became one of the major wheat-growing areas. The Gila and Salt River tribes of Pima Indians took immediately to the new grain and farmed winter wheat, then sold it back to the Sonoran Mexicans and Arizona settlers, as well as integrating it into their cosmology by beginning their new year in May, the "wheat-harvest moon." Traveling up from Sonora, wheat tortillas became *the* bread of the native Southwest, differing from locale to locale, ranging from seven to sixteen inches in diameter.

The Territory of New Mexico changed forever with the arrival of American troops after the Mexican War of 1846–48. The famous Santa Fe Trail from Missouri into New Mexico brought trade from the East, as well as Anglo settlers with their pioneer cooking on ranches and around the copper mines. The hunger for Texas beef created massive cattle drives, and cowboy or chuck wagon cuisine overseen by "cookie" was born. The post–Civil War era saw a massive influx of American settlers to the area. Rustic ranch house and mining camp baking merged Eastern and cowboy influences, with a dash of Southern cooking tempered by Creole and Cajun influences. The Army had its hardtack rations, known in the outposts by names such as teeth-dullers, bricks, and sheet iron. The Overland Stage stopped at dusty stations along its route to serve a standard fare of black coffee and corn bread.

In the 1880s, the Santa Fe Railroad arrived along with sophisticated hotel restaurant cuisine. The Harvey Houses dining facilities sprang up near the tracks, and recipes for their corn sticks still circulate. The railroad also brought the first cast-iron wood-burning stoves. In the 1920s baking was updated by another invention—the porcelain and enamel cookstove fueled by kerosene or gas.

The story of the evolution of bread leavening is as colorful as the land itself. The early Zuni produced a leaven by mixing fresh corn flour and water with chewed coarse cornmeal. This mush yeast was placed in little narrow-necked pots which were set by the hearth to ferment. Lungwort, a green tree lichen, was the basis for an overnight sponge batter. These simple yeasts were a basic ingredient in all ash cakes and fire-roasted loaves. Later, the settlers boiled potatoes and hops with sugar and salt; this mush was left to ferment and then thickened with flour a few days before using. The Natives adopted this method, cooking potatoes, cornmeal, and sugar into a stiff dough, then cutting it into squares before drying it for storage. Sourdough sponges were reconstituted from dough saved from a previous batch of dough, in the manner traditional in European baking. Commercial compressed yeast became available in the late 1800s. Quick breads known as "lightnin' breads," were leavened with *tesquesquite* (also known as *texquite),* or ground pumice rock, an early forerunner of saleratus and baking soda.

Even though contemporary Natives shop in supermarkets rather than go out to gather wild foods, many inherited food ways have come into the present intact. The revival of old ritual observances in recent years in the pueblos has reawakened a strong love of tribal lands and brought some aspects of native life into the American mainstream. The spiritual aspect of life, its ancient roots, and the culinary arts are inseparable from daily life in the Southwest. In Pueblo religions, a pinch of food was always thrown in the fire, giving back to Mother Earth and Father Sky and replenishing the source before consuming it. Food for thought as well as for body and soul.

HOLIDAYS, FIESTAS, AND INDIAN DANCES

There is another type, siki'nä, *that is round with pinched edges with small pieces on top called* flowers. *This type of bread is called* k__wói, *meaning mixed with lard. This type of bread is made for special occasions, such as ceremonials, dances, weddings, and other feasts where baskets of food are given away. In order to make the baskets of food attractive, they make these special decorative breads to include with other foods.*

SHUTES AND MELLICK, *The World of Pótsúnú: Geroninima Cruz Montoya of San Juan Pueblo* (University of New Mexico Press, 1996)

The tradition of Spanish and Mexican folk baking is still very much alive with breads baked to mark the Catholic liturgy. At the same time, the indigenous tribes living in the Southwest have their own creation stories and seasonal celebrations that respect the natural forces and guide the growing of cultivated grain and wild food crops. The holidays, fiestas, and Indian ceremonies offer a perfect way to sample the classic breads of the Southwest.

Food is central to all Catholic holidays; breads are associated with specific feast days, such as the dough skull and crossbones covering the *Pan de Muerto* for All Souls' Day or the *Rosca de los Tres Reyes,* with a china infant doll baked inside, to celebrate the Epiphany on January 6. Colonial New Mexicans fired up the outdoor oven during Easter Holy Week to bake yeast bread and panocha pudding. The ovens were blessed before using by laying a cross on the hearth and sprinkling the loaves with salt.

Cinco de Mayo is celebrated not only in Mexico but throughout the United States in Hispanic communities. Little sesame-coated buns decorated folk art fashion with names and spring greetings are prepared. The French lost the 1862 battle of Mexican independence, but their legacy of bread making has remained an integral part of Mexican cuisine, especially in the form of the crusty roll known as a Bolillo.

In northern New Mexico between Santa Fe and Taos, towns like Chimayo, Truchas, La Cienega, and Cordova or San Luis in Colorado are bastions of Hispanic adobe culture preserved intact from the conquistador period. Rancho de las Golondrinas in La Cienega, outside Santa Fe, reenacts daily Spanish colonial life and fires up the outdoor bake ovens during the Spring and Harvest Festivals.

Summer is the time for the Santa Fe Spanish and Indian outdoor markets and Old Taos Trade Fair, reenactments of the colonial trading that took place between the mountain men, local Native Americans, and Anglo and Spanish settlers. Large rounds of adobe oven yeast bread with its special crust, smoky flavor, and chewy texture, and fry breads are for sale. On Laguna Indian San José Day, also in September, festive Spanish village processions and ceremonies that have been practiced since the Spanish conquest are combined with Native dancing to honor Catholic saints. Gifts of corn and bread are laid at the feet of a statue of Saint Joseph, later to be distributed to the crowd.

The first week in July is the Santa Fe Spanish Market, an open-air bazaar. Hand-rolled soft flour tortillas are sold fresh off the *comal*. They are made with pork lard or vegetable shortening, a true sign of old-fashioned baking. The San Gerónimo Indian harvest feast is held at the end of September. The Feast of Our Lady of Guadalupe (December 10) is celebrated in most towns. She is the Spanish personification of the Madonna, Indian Mother Earth, and Corn Mother combined.

Christmas Eve is always a special time in Spanish Catholic lands, and it corresponds to the Indian winter solstice festivities. Masses are read at midnight in the missions. Christmas trees range from the evergreen to aspen, alders or white birch saplings decorated with corn husk dolls and painted bread dough ornaments. Empanadas and Indian Fruit Turnovers stuffed with dried apple or pumpkin honey are served with steaming hot chocolate and hot apple cider.

The Feast of the Epiphany merges with Governor's Day at the pueblos, accompanied by the firing up of the old ovens for feasting. February 2 is the mid-winter celebration of Candlemas, melding the European ecclesiastic feast with the colorful dances and chants honoring Native supernatural spirits. These holidays offer the full range of Mexican sweet breads, glistening with pastel-colored sugar sprinkles.

The Native American festivals are called by Hopi tribal elders when the corn crop ripens. The Hopis delegate a sunwatcher in the ancient priest-philosopher-astronomer tradition. The ceremonial year cycle is based on nine ceremonies—the first three for securing crop germination, the second three for ensuring its maturation, and the last three for celebrating the corn harvest. Each of these ceremonies has special breads associated with it.

During mid-August, the dramatic Hopi Snake Dances are held in Hotevilla and Shongopovi on Second Mesa in Arizona. Snakes are messengers to Rain Spirits and are gathered from the four directions and blessed before being released. Hopi fry bread, yeast bread, corn and flour tortillas, and blue corn finger bread, as well as the ceremonial cornmeals, are made by the village women.

Another important annual ceremony is Establishing Life Anew for All the World, which marks the winter solstice. All parts of the corn plant are used in sacred capacities during these ceremonies—stalks, leaves, pollen, kernels, and cornmeal. Kachina spirits appear and are welcomed with sprinklings of cornmeal. A sacred kernel is ceremonially planted, accompanied by prayers and songs. The fast is broken with blue piki, made in thin sheets to symbolize the flat surface of the land. A sweet blue cornmeal tamale similar to the Navajo Kneeldown Bread is served, wrapped in corn husks and tied with yucca fiber, rather like a gift.

The Southwest Rio Grande pueblos celebrate their Corn, Basket, and Rainbow Dances and festivals for springtime invocations, fertility, and preparations for planting. Pueblo ceremonies are accompanied by feasting and the ritual of baking little meat and fruit pies and yeast bread.

A wheat-based bread, called simply yeast bread, is baked in large quantities in outdoor hornos, or beehive ovens. The bread, which has remarkable keeping qualities, is distributed to friends and relatives during the ceremonies. The unique flavors that come from the smoky horno and freshly ground wheat unfortunately cannot be reproduced in a home kitchen, but the simple recipes do make wonderful home loaves.

The central pueblos at Ácoma, Isleta, and Laguna, all hold corn harvest feasts starting in late September and early October. The subterranean kivas are closed to the public, but dancing and singing is performed by village girls carrying multi-colored stalks of corn with ears attached. A ceremonial cornmeal and water mixture is kneaded into a dough and tossed out of a circle ringed with prayer-meal toward each of the cardinal directions, to be caught by the onlookers.

Many Navajo fairs are held each year at such sites as Shiprock and Window Rock, New Mexico, and Tuba City, Arizona. They include the first four days of the powerful Navajo Night Chant, a healing ceremony and dances expressing gratitude "for a good harvest to the Earth Spirit." The smell and aroma of sizzling fry bread made over open fires is everywhere in the air.

THE LANGUAGE OF MOTHER CORN

[W]afer breads were once a staple among the Pueblo people, called mowa *by the Tewa,* buwa *by the Rio Grande Tewa and* he'-we *by the Zuni, for whom a* he'-we *stone was "the rock's flesh," to be anointed with hot piñon gum and cactus juice. In* Zuni Breadstuff *(1920), Frank Cushing devoted a chapter to the wafer's many colors and kinds: a salty one flavored with lime yeast; a rich one made with milk, tasting like "cream biscuits"; a red one of red corn kernels, leaves and shoots, sweetened like "London sugar wafers"; a delicious fermented one sweetened by saliva, baked in layers between hot stones, called "buried-bread broad* he'-we."
BETTY FUSSELL, *The Story of Corn* (Knopf, 1992)

Corn has long been a staple cereal in Native, Spanish, and pioneer Southwest cuisines, and it is this continent's most famous native grain. Corn is so important that the Zuni call it *Tâ'-a,* or "the seed of seeds," and Corn Mothers are an integral part of their sacred rituals, a metaphor for daily life. Flint, or Indian corn, appears as a cultivated crop in the Southwest around 500 B.C. Archaeological evidence confirms that corn appeared as a cultivated and domesticated crop nine thousand years ago in Peru and Mexico. Corn is highly domesticated; it must be husked, shelled, planted, cultivated and hilled, fertilized, and irrigated. Unknown to Europeans, it was cultivated for thousands of years before the Spanish landed in the West Indies, and called the grain by its name in the local Arawak language, *maize.* The original strains grown by the Aztecs—Chapalote, Palomero Toluqueño Dent, and Maíz de Ocho, (eight-row soft flour corn)—are the ancestors of the hybridized corn we enjoy now.

According to legend, Yaapa, the Mockingbird, placed the different colors of corn before each tribe—the Navajo took yellow ears, the Sioux took the white, the Ute chose the flint, the Havasupai took red, the Hopi chose the smallest, stockiest ear of blue, while the Apache chose the longest ears. Traditions dictate the four compass directions in relation to colors and seasons. The Zuni believe corn reflects those colors in nature: white for the east (the spirit world); blue for the west (the sky); red, the south (fire); yellow, the north (the sun); black for the nadir (underworld); and all colors for the zenith. Legends, beliefs, and spiritual applications are attached to each color.

Corn is categorized as sweet corn (for eating off the cob), popcorn, or grinding corn, also referred to as Indian corn. Corns for grinding are distinguished by the amount and kind of starch, soft or hard, they contain. Hard-starch corns include difficult-to-grind popcorn and shiny decorative flint corn. They store well for long periods and are adapted to high altitudes. They are best ground into cornmeal by electric or water-powered grain mills. Soft-starch corns, also known as flour corns and sometimes Pueblo corn, are grown primarily in the Southwest. They are easier to grind by hand than flint corn; they are used for piki and tortillas. Dent corn, even easier to grind than flint, has a hard starch on the kernel sides and soft starch on top, which wrinkles when dried; it is the corn used for *posole* (hominy). Combination flour-flint corns, a specialty of diverse Native plant-breeding practices over the centuries, have a mixture of colors—magenta, white, blue, yellow, red, and striped—and often a mixture of types, all on one ear. Such corns are used for baking in the households that have grown them. These strains, which include Santo Domingo Mix, Hernandez Red Mix, Casados Multicolor, and Mexican June, are sometimes listed under flint corns in seed catalogs.

Native Americans developed several methods of processing dried corn. The most common, still in use, is to boil the corn with an alkali, in the form of wood ashes or slaked lime, and leave it to soak overnight. Then the corn is washed in fresh water to remove the alkali and the tough outer layer of bran is rubbed off. This corn is known as *posole* or hominy, in the Southwest. It is ground with the metate and mano into wet *masa* or *nixtamal* for tortillas. Grinding the *nixtamal* was so important a skill that a prospective bride had to demonstrate her proficiency to her future mother-in-law.

Old-style cornmeals from ground dried *posole,* or hominy, were really grits, slightly coarser than today's cornmeals; they were used for breads and porridges. The new-style cornmeals are made by grinding only the soft inner endosperm.

After the familiar yellow and white cornmeal, finely ground blue cornmeal is the next most common cornmeal in Southwest baking. One bite reveals the rich, sweet grain flavor. All colors of cornmeal can be used interchangeably in modern yeast and quick bread making. Nonhybridized strains of heirloom corn, also known as open-pollinated corn, are available to the home gardener from Native Seed/SEARCH (see page 148).

✳

The following listing is a guide to the cornmeals and flours available for baking the breads of the American Southwest.

ATOLE (See *Harina para Atole)*

BLUE CORNMEAL (See *Harina de Maíz Azul)*

[*Chicos*] CHICOS

Chicos are roasted, steamed, and dried whole kernels of Indian corn, often available in variegated colors. They are not treated with lime. This method of preservation of green corn for winter is a specialty of northern New Mexico. Although chicos may be kiln-dried on the cob, the best in terms of flavor are water-doused and pit-roasted or horno-dried overnight. They may also be pan-toasted or oven-roasted. They are used whole in a manner like *posole,* not ground into flour.
Reconstituting Chicos: Presoak and boil chicos in water as you would dried beans, or until tender.

CORN HUSKS (See *Hohas de Maíz)*

CORNMEAL (See *Harina de Maíz)*

CULINARY ASH

Made from several kinds of trees in the Southwest— Navajos prefer juniper; Hopis, chamisa (the four-winged saltbush); and Creeks, hickory—culinary ash is used in the preparation of the corn processed for tortillas. It is also mixed with water in many Native breads. The ashes are high in alkaline minerals, which increase nutritional value and enhance color in products using colored cornmeals. After burning, the clean, light pearl gray ashes that rise to the top are separated for cooking. Two tablespoons of baking soda may be substituted for each 1 cup of ash, but the finished product will not have the same nutritional value or taste. Many Native bakers have come to prefer the taste of baking soda.
Storing Culinary Ash: Store culinary ash in a tightly covered container in a cool dark place.

[Harina de Maíz] CORNMEAL

Cornmeal is ground from soft-starch, unparched whole corn kernels; it comes in fine to coarse grinds, as well as in different colors. It is used for baking powder corn breads, yeast breads, spoonbreads, pancakes, waffles, and muffins. Yellow corn is the most commonly available. White field corn is the major reservation crop in Arizona and New Mexico; it is used for prayer offerings as well as in baking for Spanish fiestas and Indian celebrations. For a light baked good, corn must be used in combination with wheat, as it contains no gluten of its own. Regular cornmeals cannot be substituted for the lime-treated *masa harina in tortillas.*

Commercial meals are ground by metal rollers that remove the germ and bran; these degerminated cornmeals have a long shelf life. For moister and more flavorful products, use stone-ground cornmeal, which contains the germ and bran.

Storing Cornmeal: Store degerminated cornmeal in an airtight container in a cool, dry place or refrigerate for 6 to 8 months. Store stone-ground cornmeals in the refrigerator for 2 to 3 months or freeze.

Toasting Cornmeal: Toasted cornmeals are known for their rich, deep flavor. Preheat the oven to 325°F. Place any color cornmeal on a baking sheet and toast, for about 20 minutes, or until very pale golden. Stir occasionally with a wooden spoon. Remove immediately from the oven and pour into a bowl to stop the toasting process, as the cornmeal can quickly become too brown and taste burnt. Toasting may also be done in a dry heavy skillet over medium heat on the stove top, stirring constantly. Let toasted cornmeal cool before adding to a recipe.

Parching and Grinding Dried Corn: Buy whole blue, red, white, or yellow dried corn kernels at a local natural foods store, through mail order, or obtain homegrown, which will need to be shelled and washed in running water. Place in a cast-iron skillet over low heat on top of the stove and stir constantly with a wooden spoon until the kernels are golden brown and smell a bit like popcorn, about 20 minutes. (The corn may also be parched in a preheated 350°F. oven.) Cool slightly and grind while a bit warm in the grinding attachment of a heavy-duty electric mixer, a hand-powered corn mill, or an electric or hand grain grinder, to the desired texture. Store in a tightly covered container in a cool place for up to 3 months.

[Harina de Maíz Azul] BLUE CORNMEAL

Blue cornmeal is ground from blue corn; it is a bit grainier and less starchy than white and yellow cornmeal. When baked, blue cornmeal has a dull purple-gray color and earthy flavor. When culinary ash is added, the blue color becomes very distinct. Blue cornmeal is a mandatory part of Navajo wedding ceremonies and Hopi religious practices. It was regarded as the most nutritious corn and was fed to pregnant and lactating women.

Originally available only in northern New Mexico and grown locally by the Natives, blue cornmeal is now widely available in specialty food stores and by mail order. Use blue cornmeal in place of regular yellow and white cornmeals. Blue cornmeal needs a bit more fat when substituted for yellow or white cornmeal. Lime-treated blue cornmeal, also known as *harinilla* (see page 20), is used exclusively for tortillas.

Grinding Blue Cornmeal: See Parching and Grinding Dried Corn (left).

[Harina de Maíz Rojo] RED CORNMEAL

Red cornmeal is prepared and used like blue cornmeal; it is becoming more widely available.

[Harina para Atole] ATOLE

Atole is flour ground from fresh, not lime-treated, blue corn kernels that have been roasted. The flour, finer than regular cornmeal, is often labeled *harina para atole* or *masa de maíz para atole.* It can be used in breads when very fine cornmeal is desired. The finest grade is cured by smoking and roasting in wood-fired adobe ovens, although most of the flour is kiln dried. The corn is then lava-wheel ground. When a bread recipe calls for regular blue cornmeal, you can substitute atole; many bakers prefer it. Use in 50-50 with wheat flour for best results.

Making Atole from Regular Blue Cornmeal: Preheat the oven to 375°F. Spread the blue cornmeal on an ungreased baking sheet. Toast in the center of the oven, stirring at least twice for even browning, for about 10 minutes.

Atole is most commonly used to prepare a home breakfast drink of the same name (also called *ator)* that dates back to pre-Columbian America. The roasted blue corn flour is mixed with water and salt, and boiled until thick. A porridge rather like a runny Cream of Wheat, which the Pueblos call *chackewe,* is also made. When the atole is mixed with Mexican hot chocolate it is called *champurrado.*

Atole Breakfast Drink: Combine 1½ cups water and 1½ cups milk in a small saucepan. Add ½ cup roasted fine blue cornmeal and heat slowly over medium heat, stirring constantly. Add ¼ teaspoon salt and honey or maple syrup to taste. Simmer for 5 minutes, or until creamy. Serve hot. Serves 2.

[Harinilla] ROASTED BLUE CORN FLOUR

Much finer than regular corn meal, *harinilla* is used exclusively for making blue corn tortillas. In contrast to *harina de maíz azul,* which is ground from untreated corn, *harinilla* is known for its capricious, crumbly nature in baking and is often combined with some fine white or yellow *masa harina* to help it hold together. It can be used up to 50-50 with wheat flour for yeast breads when a strong smoky flavor

is desired. Do not use exclusively for quick breads or pancakes, as it is too fine. *Harinilla* is also sometimes labeled *harinia.*

[Hojas de Maíz] CORN HUSKS

Dried corn husks are the traditional wrappings for steamed tamales or cooking baskets; they can be used to cradle muffins and yeast breads as well.
Reconstituting Dried Corn Husks: Rinse and remove the silks and soak in warm water until pliable, about 1 hour. (Corn husks are inedible.)

HOMINY (see *Posole)*

[Masa] DOUGH

Masa (dough in Spanish, corn dough in Mexican) refers to the doughs used for making tortillas, such as *masa de harina* (wheat dough), *Masa de trigo* (whole wheat dough), or *masa de maíz* (corn dough). Damp slaked corn is ground traditionally by hand on a *metate* with a *mano.* The finer the *masa* is ground, the smoother the finished texture of the tortillas will be. *Masa preparada para tortillas* is a premixed ready-to-use wet dough with water and lard added, not to be confused with regular *masa,* which is simply ground corn. Fresh cornmeal *masa* is available in Mexican groceries or from a tortilla factory. It is highly perishable. It will keep in the refrigerator for about 2 days before losing elasticity and souring. (Fresh cornmeal *masa* may be frozen for up to 1 month.)

[Masa Harina] INSTANT CORN FLOUR TORTILLA MIX

Masa Harina is the registered trademark of an instant corn flour tortilla mix ground from fresh corn *masa* that has been dried and ground. It was developed and marketed by the Quaker Oats company at the Mexican government's request. Other nationally distributed brands include Goya and Maseca (packaged in Mexico). Similar mixes are marketed by other mills as Tortilla Masa, Horina Preparada

Para Tortillas, or Instant Corn Masa Mix *(Masa Instantanea de Maíz)*. If a recipe calls for instant *masa,* this is the ingredient it requires. Coarse grinds are used for tamales *(masa harina para tamales)* and fine grinds for tortillas *(masa harina para tortillas).*

Plain *masa harina* is often available stone-ground from white, blue, or yellow corn. It comes in both grinds. Recipes in this book call for masa harina para tortillas for tortillas. It can also be used as an ingredient in yeast breads when mixed with all-purpose or high gluten bread flour as well as in quick corn breads. The blue corn mix contains a small amount of white or yellow corn to help hold the tortilla together.

NIXTAMAL (See *Posole*)

[Posole] HOMINY

Also known in New Mexico by nixtamal, this is kernels of field corn that are cooked and soaked in an alkali solution to soften and swell the hard dent corn. This process is known as hominying. It was known to the pre-Columbian Indians as *nixtamil.* The corn becomes chewy, flavorful, and easy to digest. The process also increases the nutritional value of the corn by adjusting the amino acid balance. After hominying, the corn is ground for *masa* or dried whole for storage. Hominy is available from white, yellow, and blue corn. Recipes for hominying appear in cookbooks as diverse as Diana Kennedy's *Art of Mexican Cooking* to early editions of the *Joy of Cooking.* When dried and coarsely cracked, hominy is called grits; when dried and finely ground it is called *masa harina,* literally dough flour. Hominy comes dried, canned, or frozen. Fresh, partially cooked frozen, and dried hominy all need to be cooked before using. Do not add any salt, or the kernels will not soften. Canned white or yellow hominy, drained and rinsed before using, can be substituted.

MAKING HOMINY
MAKES ABOUT 4 CUPS HOMINY

1 pound (about 2½ cups) dried dent or flint corn
    kernels, yellow, blue, red, or white
2 teaspoons slaked lime or ¼ cup culinary ashes
    (See Note)

Rinse the corn in cold water and drain. In a nonreactive saucepan, cover the corn with 4 cups water. Dissolve the lime in 1 cup water. It will bubble up. When it stops, add to the corn and stir. Bring to a low simmer and cook for 1 hour. Do not boil. Remove from the heat and let stand in the liquid overnight. The skins will slip off when rubbed. Grind in a food processor to make fresh *masa* ready immediately to make tortillas. Keeps wrapped in plastic in the refrigerator for about 4 days.

Note: Slaked lime (calcium hydroxide powder) is available in hardware stores, pharmacies, or tortillerias, or buy a chunk of calcium hydroxide *(cal)* at a Mexican grocery; 1 tablespoon baking soda may be substituted.

Cooking Hominy: Rinse 1 pound fresh or frozen hominy or ¾ pound dried hominy in a large sieve under cold running water. Discard any discolored kernels. Place in a nonreactive saucepan and cover by 2 inches with cold water. Bring to a boil, reduce the heat to a simmer, and cook fresh or frozen hominy for about 1 to 1½ hours, dried hominy for up to 3 hours, or until tender and the kernels burst open, but still slightly firm to the bite. Remove from the heat and drain off most of the liquid, reserving it for another dish. Let cool to room temperature. (May be stored, covered, in the refrigerator for up to 2 days.)

RED CORNMEAL (see *Harina de Maíz Rojo*)

OLD

SOUTHWEST

BAKERY

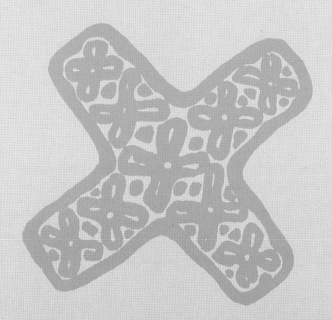

Joy and Beauty,
may the sweet yellow maize accompany you
to the ends of the earth.
NAVAJO MEDICINE PRAYER

All Southwestern tribes ate flatbreads, and specific areas of their dwellings were devoted to food preparation. Apache bands lived in *wikiups,* a type of easily moved brush shelter with a single room floor plan, which had an open hearth in the center and a food preparation area to the side, similar to the Navajo hogan. During the summer, the *wikiup* had an outdoor arbor, with space for tortilla making.

The Pima and Papago along the Gila and Salt Rivers, some of the hottest desert areas in the Southwest, grew food on the river banks and situated their villages near the fields. They lived in *kis,* domed mud-covered brush shelters, during the winter, and in arbors framed in cornstalks for wind breaks in the summer. The hearth and bread preparation area, usually for tortillas and ash breads, were under a shade arbor. The most primitive method for baking dough is to bury it in the embers of an outdoor fire. Granaries were often situated on the kis roof, and community food was in storage buildings built of woven straw. *Kis* are no longer lived in today; reservation wood and adobe mud houses have modern kitchens.

The Navajo family hogan, an octagonal one-room dwelling, is divided into male and female sides, with the food, kitchen, and weaving equipment on the female side. The fire pit or hearth is in the center, the heart of the house, with a smoke hole in the center of the roof. Many households still have wood-burning cook stoves in the center for heating and baking; some also have a gas stove for cooking. Meats, fry bread, and tortillas are often cooked outside because of the smoke and grease.

The pueblo adobe village dwellers had houses with adjoining rooms dictated by clan relationships. Since the first floor was half underground and cool, it was used for food storage, with the upper rooms used for food preparation. Smoke flues traveled upward to the roof terrace from interior *fogons,* or corner stoves, where there were racks for drying corn, meat jerky, pinto bean pods, and winter squash. The Spanish introduced the *fogon* to the pueblo tribes to replace the old center-floor open hearths. The Indians added flues and chimney pots for more efficient release of the smoke and a suspended smoke hood over the fire. An outdoor *horno,* often framed with drying sunflower stalks, was an area for summer cooking.

Indoor food preparation rooms included areas for pottery storage containers with stone lids; niches for religious items, such as sacred cornmeals; and stacks of dried corn cobs in close proximity to the grinding stones. Sacks were filled with hand-gathered wild acorns and piñon (pine nuts). Yucca and cedar baskets served for piki trays and for winnowing and sifting grain. A flat earthenware *comal* was used for toasting cornmeal and making corn-based flatbreads. There was a special area for burning culinary ashes. Cooking utensils were hung from the rafters and walls. Overhead, prayer feathers hung alongside dried corn husks, wild herbs, and hand-gathered leaves for teas.

An old Native Pueblo kitchen was equipped to cook many kinds of corn–steamed breads, atole (see page 20), porridges, and sweet corn, as well as popcorn. Early food preparation areas had a center-floor hearth for cooking, with piles of splintered piñon, juniper, cedar, cornstalks, and sagebrush materials for burning.

Smooth stone slabs fit over the fire for piki making. A specialty bread, piki is as thin as tissue and made in a variety of colors, such as pink, blue, or yellow, and flavors, including chile. Sometimes it is colored by adding such ingredients as ground coxcomb flowers or safflower. An Indian girl was not considered ready for marriage until she had mastered the art of piki making—slathering the corn gruel onto the hot rock with bare fingers with just the right touch. Once a staple, piki is still mandatory for Hopi ceremonies, and the women spend hours in the cabin room designated just for making this bread.

Grinding areas to make cornmeals include wooden bins to catch the flour as it is ground, and four or five sloping rectangular *metate* grinding stones of varying degrees of roughness. The flours pass along one from the other to grind ever finer textures. A grass brush collects the meal into a pile, which is ground with a small stone rolling pin, a *mano*. Shallow wooden basins hold water and moist *posole* (hominy) for grinding into *masa* dough for tortillas and other types of corn breads. At the turn of the century, many homes began using hand-turned coffee mills for grinding the hard dried corn kernels more quickly. Although electric grain mills are popular for daily breads, the hand-milling techniques practiced by the older tribal women are mandatory for ceremonial breads even today.

The old Southwest Bakery also includes traditional and innovative recipes for tortilla slapbreads and Old World Mexican Breads. The recipes in this chapter illuminate a long-standing culinary tradition.

Because of the diverse cultural groups of the area, they need to be consistently described. American Indians tend to refer to themselves as Native American, Indian, or by tribe such as Apache or Pueblo. Those people descendent of the Spanish or Spanish speakers are Hispanic or Spanish. For the purposes of this book, those who are neither Indian or Spanish are referred to as Anglos.

Luckily for the modern baker, ancient techniques such as outdoor baking are not always necessary to prepare traditional breads.

Bakers work with an artist's acumen and techniques that have not altered in centuries. These breads are every bit as wonderful to make today as when they were first made, and are easy to reproduce authentically in the home kitchen.

TORTILLAS:
SOUTHWEST DAILY BREAD

It requires a much-practiced hand to manage the dough. Few now know how to make the corn tortilla, as preparing the corn takes a great deal of time and labor. If making out of dry nixtamal meal, mix meal with hot water, cover, and let stand five minutes, so it will stick together, or use fresh dough. Take a piece of the dough the size of a biscuit, work between hands into a round, thin cake. Lay this on a greased, hot iron. (A little rag dipped in melted pork lard is used to grease iron.) Wet the hand in cold water often, and press and whirl tortilla around continually to keep from sticking. When flattened thin and smooth, and cooked on the under side, wet the hand and press edge of palm on one end of the tortilla and turn it quickly. Let brown and place spread in a basket to keep from getting soggy.
Cleofas M. Jaramillo, *Genuine New Mexico Tasty Recipes* (Ancient City Press, reprinted 1981)

There is such a thing as a tortilla education. Native traditions give respect to this humble flatbread—and you will too when you mix that first batch of dough and try to get it to hold together properly! Tortillas, the staple bread of the pre-Spanish Southwest, were made from a wet mass of freshly ground corn that had been treated with lime, which softened the tough hulls and released niacin. When the Spanish settled in the Southwest, they brought wheat, and the corn tortilla soon had a sibling that was flakier and more pliable because of the stretchy nature of the gluten in the wheat flour. They called both kinds of flatbreads "tortilla," Spanish for "little cake." This is a bread that really shows if it is made by the human hand or not. A homemade tortilla still reigns supreme. Whether it is a corn tortilla patted by hand or a flour tortilla rolled out with a rolling pin, a handmade tortilla is much trickier than it looks. Practice and observation as well as equipment are important. You will need a press, a rolling pin, and a griddle. Hand patting corn tortillas is much more work than it looks; a metal hand press really comes to the rescue. Some connoisseurs swear by using two griddles at the same time, with one a bit hotter than the other, so that each side bakes at a different temperature. This technique demands a smooth rhythm of synchronized movements. Home bakers mostly cook the breads on an ungreased griddle or outside on a makeshift grill.

You can prepare your own corn dough (several recipes follow), or you can buy plain fresh *masa* dough or *masa preparada para tortillas* (premixed with lard, salt, and water) or by the pound at a Mexican market. With a minimal amount of fuss you can press out and bake your own tortillas.

UNDERSTANDING TORTILLAS
✳ Be sure to read The Language of Mother Corn (see pages 17–21) to distinguish the terms used in purchasing and preparing corn doughs and flours.
✳ *Masa Harina,* an instant corn tortilla mix, is sold in five-pound bags like flour. It is not the same as polenta or regular cornmeal, which cannot be substituted in tortilla making. You can also use *masa harina para tortillas.* Both are

widely available in supermarkets in the flour section or in Hispanic markets, or you can order them by mail. Some bakers mix their own combination of *masa harina*.

✳ Assemble your ingredients and equipment before mixing the doughs for most efficient use of space and time. For the seasoning and care of your griddle, see page 145. Cut three sets of heavy plastic wrap (some bakers use wax paper or heavy plastic sandwich bags cut in half) for rolling and pressing. A batch of homemade tortillas takes about 1½ hours to mix, shape, and bake.

✳ Tortilla dough can be mixed by hand, in a heavy-duty electric mixer, or in a food processor. It must be moist enough to shape, yet dry enough to bake on the griddle. Add most of the liquid called for in a corn tortilla recipe, then slowly add the rest for control over consistency. Corn dough is almost indestructible, although proper consistency is important. If it is too dry, add more water; if too moist, correct with more flour. If the dough is too dry, the uncooked tortilla will have a ragged edge. If the dough is too moist, it will stick to the plastic.

✳ Immediately wrap stacks of baked tortillas in a clean dish towel until cooled. This keeps them moist and soft as the steam evaporates.

✳ Store cooled tortillas airtight in plastic wrap. They can be refrigerated for up to 5 days, or frozen for up to 2 months.

MAKING THE DOUGH IN A FOOD PROCESSOR: Recipes in this chapter give instructions for making tortilla dough by hand or in a heavy-duty mixer. To use a food processor, combine the dry ingredients in the workbowl. Add the fat (if called for) and process until just blended and crumbly; do not overprocess. Add the water slowly through the feed tube and process until a soft ball is formed, about 10 seconds. Remove from the bowl and knead a few times to smooth the dough.

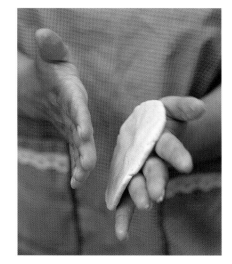

FORMING CORN TORTILLAS: To form by hand, wet your hands and roll a small egg-size piece of dough (1½ inches in diameter) into a ball. Holding your palms and fingers straight, quickly and gently pat the dough into a flat round by shifting the dough back and forth between your palms, turning one hand 90 degrees after each pat until a thin cake is formed. This makes for a thicker tortilla with more ragged edges than if you use a press. Trim the edges with a knife or pot lid with a sharp edge to form perfect rounds. Practice is the key here.

To form using an iron or wood press, place the ball of dough between 2 sheets of plastic wrap. Never press out a tortilla directly on the surface of the press. Flatten in degrees, with the greatest flattening done toward the hinge side of the press. Turn to create an even thickness. If baking immediately, open the press and carefully peel off the plastic. Pick up the tortilla and gently flip it over onto your other hand and fingers to peel off the bottom layer of plastic before placing on the griddle, or pile the tortillas between sheets of plastic wrap, until ready to bake. (The tortillas may be refrigerated for up to 8 hours before baking.) Any misshapen rounds or scraps can be worked back into the ball of dough and reshaped.

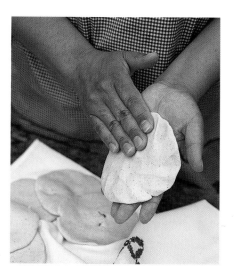

FORMING FLOUR TORTILLAS: Let flour tortilla dough rest before rolling out, to allow the stretchy gluten to relax. Pinch off pieces of dough and let them rest. Roll out the ball in the manner of a pie crust dough, rolling from the center out and making quarter turns on a very lightly flour-dusted work surface. Never roll all the way to the edge. Expect some wonderfully funny shapes to emerge when you are beginning. (Seasoned tortilla makers are able to roll out 3 tortillas at a time, no small feat to the uninitiated.) Drape the tortilla over your hand and gently lower one edge, then roll it off your hand onto the hot griddle to avoid wrinkles and overlapping of the dough. Slide off a plate, if necessary.

BAKING TORTILLAS: Use a heavy cast-iron skillet, griddle, or *comal* that can take the constant high temperature needed for baking. Temperature is critical. Heat the skillet over medium-high heat until a drop of water dances across the surface. Overbaked tortillas are stiff; lower the heat slightly and reduce baking time as necessary by 10-second intervals. The first side, called *la raspada,* can be peeled off. Grasp the edge of the tortilla with your thumb and forefinger to turn. The second side bakes up with brown spots and dry edges, like a crepe. Do not use a spatula. The exception here is for blue corn tortillas which have a tendency to stick. If tortillas stick while baking, scrape the accumulated grit clean with a metal spatula before proceeding.

REHEATING HOMEMADE TORTILLAS: Preheat the oven to 400°F. Place individual tortillas directly on the rack and bake 2 to 3 minutes, or until soft and pliable. Wrap stacks of eight at a time in aluminum foil. Or place a stack in a terra cotta tortilla warmer and heat at 350°F. for about 15 minutes, depending on the size of the stack.
On a cast-iron skillet, griddle, or comal: Heat an ungreased pan over medium-high heat until hot. Place a tortilla on the surface and leave just until puffy, about 10 seconds. Turn once. Use a tablespoon of oil if a crisp tortilla is desired.

On a stove top grill or grill: Heat the grill or charcoal fire to medium-high to hot heat. Place a tortilla on the surface and leave just until puffy. Turn once.
In a microwave oven: Place individual tortillas in a single layer on the microwave turntable and warm just until puffy, about 30 seconds. Or wrap stacks in plastic wrap and microwave at 2-minute intervals, or until the stack is warm and pliable.
In a bamboo steamer: Wrap a stack of tortillas in a clean dish towel and place in a vegetable steamer basket over an inch of boiling water. Cover and steam 5 to 8 minutes, or until the stack is warm and pliable.

CORN TORTILLAS

Tortillas de Maíz

The dried cornmeal specifically used for tortillas, masa harina para tortillas, *has a distinctive limey taste; it is ground to a fine powdery flour. Corn tortillas are traditionally patted into rounds by hand or flattened in a tortilla press.*

MAKES EIGHTEEN 7-INCH TORTILLAS

4 cups yellow or white *masa harina para tortillas,*
    preferably stone-ground
½ teaspoon salt
2⅔ cups hot water

1] In a medium mixing bowl using your hands or a wooden spoon, or in the bowl of a heavy-duty electric mixer fitted with the paddle attachment, combine the *masa harina para tortillas,* salt, and most of the water. (To use a food processor, see page 28). Mix thoroughly until evenly moistened and the mixture forms a firm springy ball, adding a teaspoon of water at a time if the dough seems too dry, or more *masa harina* if too wet. Cover with a clean damp dishtowel or plastic wrap and let rest for 1 hour at room temperature. Keep covered while pressing or rolling out the tortillas. If using later, wrap the entire ball of dough in plastic wrap and refrigerate for up to 24 hours.

2] To shape the tortillas, divide into 18 equal portions about the size of a golf ball. Place one of the portions of the dough between 2 pieces of plastic wrap or wax paper. Press in a tortilla press, turning at regular intervals, until the desired thickness. Often the edges will crack; you can leave them like this, or press on the plastic to smooth, or trim with a knife. Leave in the plastic wrap until ready to cook. The pile of tortillas may be refrigerated for up to 8 hours before baking.

3] To bake the tortillas, heat an ungreased heavy cast-iron skillet, griddle, or *comal* over medium-high heat until drops of water sprinkled on the surface dance across it. Peel off both layers of the plastic and place each tortilla onto the hot pan, one at a time, or as many that will fit without touching. Bake for 30 seconds on the first side, turn over, and bake for 1 minute. Turn back to the first side and bake for a final 30 seconds. The tortilla will puff up and be speckled with brown spots. The tortillas can be baked in advance, stacked, wrapped in plastic or placed in a thick plastic bag, and refrigerated overnight. Reheat as needed right before serving (see page 30).

31

BLUE CORN TORTILLAS

Tortillas de Maíz Azul

A specialty of northern New Mexico, blue corn tortillas are an earthy color with a strong corn flavor. It's worth searching out harinilla *for these tortillas. Eat blue corn tortillas the day they are baked; use the day-olds in enchilada casseroles.*

This recipe was developed by food writer Jacquie Higuera McMahan. She and I agree that some special breads may require the touch of a Native baker to be executed properly, to have the "taste of a woman's hands," but this nontraditional recipe comes very close to that.

MAKES TWELVE 5-INCH TORTILLAS

1 cup blue corn *harinilla* or *masa harina para tortillas*
¾ cup yellow or white *masa harina para tortillas*
¼ cup unbleached all-purpose flour or bread flour
¼ teaspoon salt
1 cup minus 1 tablespoon hot water

1] In a medium mixing bowl using your hands or a wooden spoon, or in the bowl of a heavy-duty electric mixer fitted with the paddle attachment, combine the *harinilla,* the *masa harina para tortillas,* salt, and most of the water (to use a food processor, see page 28). Mix thoroughly until evenly moistened and the mixture forms a firm springy ball, not sticky. If too dry, add a teaspoonful of water at a time. Cover with a clean damp dishtowel or plastic wrap and let rest for 1 hour at room temperature. Keep covered while pressing or rolling out the tortillas as the blue corn dough dries out quickly.

2] Divide the dough into 12 portions and shape into 5-inch rounds as in Step 2 of Corn Tortillas (page 31).

3] To bake, heat an ungreased heavy cast-iron skillet, griddle, or *comal* over medium-high heat until drops of water sprinkled on the surface dance across it. Peel off both layers of the plastic wrap and immediately place each tortilla onto the hot pan one at a time, as many as will fit without touching. Bake for 30 seconds on the first side, release the tortilla with a thin metal spatula if it sticks, turn over, and bake for another 30 seconds. When the tortilla puffs up, press down immediately with a folded towel. It will be speckled with brown spots. Wrap in a clean dishtowel until needed. Best eaten within 1 hour.

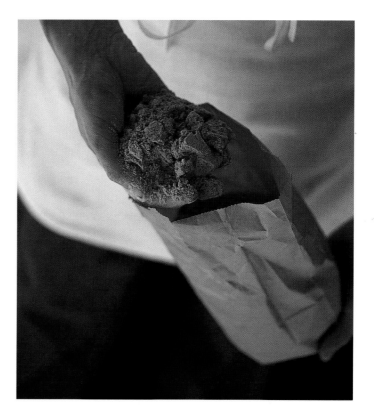

NIXTAMAL TORTILLAS

The delightful cookbook The Well-Filled Tortilla by Victoria Wise and Susanna Hoffman (Workman, 1990) includes a special masa dough recipe that uses canned or fresh cooked hominy, sometimes called nixtamal, to moisten it. This technique, as the Well-Filled writers acknowledge, was developed by food writer Betty Fussell. The whole hominy adds a dimension quite like fresh Native-ground doughs and makes the dough exceptionally malleable. It is quickly mixed in the food processor, a modern alternative to hand grinding.

MAKES TWENTY 6-INCH TORTILLAS

1½ cups (about one 29-ounce can) drained, canned
    hominy or fresh cooked hominy (see page 21)
1½ cups yellow or white *masa harina para tortillas*,
    preferably stone-ground
¼ teaspoon salt
1 cup hot water

1] Place the hominy in a food processor and add the *masa harina para tortillas,* salt, and most of the water. Process until the dough forms a soft firm ball, about 10 seconds. Remove from the food processor and knead briefly to smooth the dough. Cover with a clean damp dishtowel or plastic wrap and let rest for 1 hour at room temperature. Keep covered while pressing or rolling out the tortillas. (The ball of dough may be wrapped in plastic wrap and refrigerated for up to 24 hours.)

2] Divide the dough into 20 portions and shape into 6-inch rounds, pressing out as in Step 2 of Corn Tortillas (page 31). Bake the tortillas as in Step 3.

FLOUR TORTILLAS
Tortillas de Harina

Although all traditional recipes for flour tortillas call for a solid fat, you can use oil (see the variation that follows). To keep the traditional flaky texture, freeze part of the flour with the oil. This technique was developed in the Eating Well magazine test kitchens and shared with me by Jacquie McMahan. The trick of forming the dough ball into a mushroom shape comes from native Texan food writer Elaine Corn. Some Spanish recipes call for evaporated milk to be substituted for half of the water.

MAKES FIFTEEN 8- TO 9-INCH TORTILLAS

4 cups unbleached all-purpose flour
1½ teaspoons baking powder
1½ teaspoons salt
½ cup solid vegetable shortening, butter,
    bacon drippings, or lard
1½ cups warm water

1] In a medium mixing bowl using your hands or a wooden spoon or in the bowl of a heavy-duty electric mixer fitted with the paddle attachment on the lowest setting, combine the flour, baking powder, and salt. Cut in the fat until crumbly, using a fork or pastry blender if making by hand. Gradually add the warm water to the flour mixture, stirring just until the dough sticks together, clears the sides of the bowl, and forms a soft ball. Too much water makes a tough tortilla, so proceed slowly. Give the dough a few kneads (fewer than 10, no longer than 1 minute) to make a smooth ball (often described as earlobe soft) that is no longer sticky. Form into a cylinder and wrap the dough in plastic wrap or a clean dishtowel to prevent drying out. Let rest at room temperature for at least 30 minutes or up to 2 hours, until slightly puffy and shiny.

2] To shape the tortillas, divide the dough into 15 equal portions. Shape each into a ball and place on a baking sheet or marble slab. Let the balls rest for 20 to 30 minutes more. Drape each ball around your forefinger, making a depression on the underside. This makes a mushroom shape and creates an air bubble, which helps it roll out into an even round. On a very lightly floured work surface, flatten the ball with your palm (the balls can rest on a greased baking sheet, covered tightly, for another 30 minutes, if necessary, at this point). With a *palote* or thin rolling pin,

roll each ball out from the center to the edge but without pressing on the edge, lifting the dough and giving it a quarter turn several times, to form a thin round 8 to 9 inches in diameter, depending on the size of your griddle. Trim the ragged edges and using a dry pastry brush, dust off any extra flour, if necessary. Stack between layers of plastic wrap to prevent drying out while rolling out the remaining dough. You can store the rounds in the refrigerator for up to 6 hours before baking, if necessary, but baking immediately is best.

3] To bake the tortillas, heat an ungreased heavy cast-iron skillet, griddle, or *comal* over medium-high heat until drops of water sprinkled on the surface dance across it. Place the tortillas, one at a time, or as many as will fit without overlapping in the pan, and bake for 30 seconds. The tortilla will form bubbles; press them down gently with a spatula or folded towel and slightly twist. When you see the bubbles, turn over to the other side and bake for 30 seconds, or until the dough looks dry and brown spots are formed and the tortilla is soft, but not crisp. It is easy to overbake, so take care with the timing. Remove each tortilla to a clean towel or stack between layers of plastic wrap. If not serving right away, wrap in plastic or place in a thick plastic bag when cool. Refrigerate no longer than overnight. Rewarm as needed right before eating (see page 30).

VARIATIONS
Low-fat Flour Tortillas: Prepare the flour, baking soda, and salt mixture. Blend ½ cup vegetable or olive oil with ½ cup of the flour mixture and freeze for 2 hours in a tightly covered plastic freezer container. Substitute this mixture for the solid fat in Step 1. Proceed with Steps 2 and 3. Makes 15 tortillas.

Mesquite Flour Tortillas: Substitute 1 cup mesquite flour (see page 35) for 1 cup of the all-purpose flour.

SONORAN FLOUR TORTILLAS

Any flour tortilla can be stretched to a large diameter. Some that are one to two feet in diameter are baked in rural areas on surfaces as unusual as a scrubbed manhole cover or oil drum lid. Large ultra-thin rounds are the specialty of Sonoran bakers in southern Arizona. The tortilla dough is gently stretched in a manner like strudel dough, or hung over the fist and pulled and spun like pizza dough. Since unbaked large tortillas are delicate to handle, become adept at handling regular flour tortillas first. Make sure you have a cooking surface large enough (a 14-inch cast-iron skillet or iron comal is perfect) and remember that the thinner the tortilla, the faster it bakes.

MAKES TWELVE 12-INCH TORTILLAS

4 cups unbleached all-purpose flour or bread flour
1½ teaspoons salt
⅓ cup solid vegetable shortening, butter,
    soy margarine, or lard
1½ cups warm water

1] In a medium mixing bowl using your hands or a wooden spoon or in the bowl of a heavy-duty electric mixer fitted with the paddle attachment on the lowest setting, combine the flour and salt. Cut in the shortening until crumbly, using a fork or pastry blender if making by hand. Gradually add the warm water to the flour mixture, stirring just until the dough sticks together, clears the sides of the bowl, and forms a soft ball. Too much water makes a tough tortilla, so proceed slowly; this dough needs to be as soft as possible without being sticky. Give the dough a few kneads (fewer than 10, no longer than 1 minute) to make a smooth ball. Form into a cylinder and wrap the dough in plastic wrap or a clean dishtowel to prevent drying out. Let rest at room temperature for 45 minutes, or until slightly puffy and shiny. (The dough may be coated with a film of oil, wrapped in plastic, and refrigerated for up to 12 hours or overnight.)

2] To shape the tortillas, divide the dough into 12 equal portions. Shape each into a ball and place on a baking sheet or marble slab. Drape each ball around your forefinger, making a depression on the underside. This makes a mushroom shape and creates an air bubble, which helps it roll out into an even round. On a very lightly floured work surface, flatten the ball with your palm. (The flattened balls can rest on a greased baking sheet, covered tightly, for another 30 minutes, if necessary at this point.) Roll out each ball from the center to the edge, without pressing on the edge, lifting the dough and giving it a quarter turn several times, into a thin 10-inch round. Continue to stretch the dough into a 12-inch round by gently stretching with your fingertips and stroking from the center out to the edges a few times. Trim the ragged edges and using a dry pastry brush, dust off any extra flour, if necessary. Stack between layers of plastic wrap to prevent drying out while rolling out the remaining dough. Bake as soon as possible.

3] To bake the tortillas, heat a 12- to 14-inch ungreased heavy cast-iron skillet or *comal* over medium-high heat until drops of water sprinkled on the surface dance across it. Place the tortillas, one at a time, in the pan, and bake for 30 seconds. Leave any bubbles that form alone. When the dough looks dry and brown spots are formed, turn over to the other side and bake for 30 seconds more. Keep flipping back and forth until the tortilla is soft, but not crisp. It is very easy to overbake such a thin tortilla, so pay close attention to the timing. Remove each tortilla to a clean towel and fold it in quarters. Cover until serving.

PUEBLO INDIAN WHOLE WHEAT TORTILLAS

Tortillas de Harina de Trigo

The combination of whole wheat or panocha flour (sprouted wheat flour) and white flour is common in Pueblo Indian baking. When you see the term trigo *you will know the recipe will call for some whole wheat flour. These tortillas are rolled a bit thicker than other flour tortillas. The sugar tortillas are good for dessert with jam or Cajeta Spread (page 131), or used day-old in a bread pudding.*

MAKES TWENTY 8- TO 9-INCH TORTILLAS

4 cups unbleached all-purpose flour

2 cups panocha, whole wheat flour, or graham flour

2 teaspoons salt

1½ tablespoons baking powder

½ cup solid vegetable shortening, butter, bacon grease, chicken fat, or lard

2 cups warm water, warm non-fat milk, part evaporated skim milk, or evaporated goat's milk

1] In a medium mixing bowl using your hands or a wooden spoon, or in the bowl of a heavy-duty electric mixer fitted with the paddle attachment on the lowest setting, combine the flours, salt, and baking powder. Cut in the fat until crumbly, using a fork or pastry blender if making by hand. Gradually add the warm water or milk, stirring just until the dough sticks together, clears the sides of the bowl, and forms a soft ball. Too much liquid makes a tough tortilla, so proceed slowly. Give the dough a few kneads (fewer than 10, no longer than 1 minute) to make a smooth ball (often described as earlobe soft) that is no longer sticky. Cover the dough ball with a clean dishtowel or plastic wrap to prevent drying out. Let rest for at least 30 minutes or up to 2 hours, or until slightly puffy and shiny.

2] Divide the dough into 20 portions and shape into 8- to 9-inch rounds, rolling out as in Step 2 of Flour Tortillas (page 35). Bake the tortillas as in Step 3.

VARIATION

Pueblo Indian Sugar Tortillas: Add ¼ cup sugar to the flour mixture and increase the shortening or other fat to ½ cup.

APACHE TORTILLAS

Sixte

The Apache tortilla is a small thick round made without any fat. On the reservation, they were baked on a hot grill, griddle, or even scrubbed plow disks, over an open fire. This recipe is adapted from Good Bread *by Barbara Joan Hansen (Macmillan, 1976), a wonderful bread book.*

MAKES TWELVE 5-INCH TORTILLAS

2¾ cups unbleached all-purpose flour

¼ cup amaranth flour

2 teaspoons salt

1 teaspoon baking powder

1 cup warm water

1] In a medium bowl, combine the flours, salt, and baking powder. Make a well in the center and pour in the warm water. Work with your hands or a wooden spoon into a stiff dough. If the dough is too dry, add more water by the teaspoonful. Turn the dough out onto a lightly floured work surface and knead a few times to make a smooth ball that is not sticky. Cover the dough with plastic wrap and let rest for 30 minutes.

2] Divide the dough into 12 equal portions and form each into a ball or oval. Flatten each portion slightly and cover while rolling them out. Using a rolling pin, form 5-inch rounds ½ inch thick (as in Step 2 in Flour Tortillas). Or use a tortilla press. Trim the ragged edges and using a dry pastry brush, dust off any extra flour, if necessary. Stack between layers of plastic wrap to prevent drying. (The stack may be stored, well wrapped, in the refrigerator for up to 8 hours.)

3] To bake the tortillas, heat an ungreased heavy cast-iron skillet, griddle, or *comal* over medium-high heat until drops of water sprinkled on the surface dance across it. Place the tortillas, one at a time, on the griddle. They will cook quickly. Cook 1 to 1½ minutes, or until the baked side becomes speckled with brown. Do not overbake, or the tortilla will be stiff. Turn it over and bake for the same length of time as on the first side. Transfer the hot tortillas from the griddle into a basket lined with a clean dry towel. Cool and store the tortillas in heavy plastic sandwich bags.

MULTI-GRAIN TORTILLAS

These are modern-day corn and flour tortillas, updated with some flavorful specialty flour added. Amaranth flour melds exceptionally well with the flavor of corn flour. Wild amaranth grain was widely used by Apache and northern Mexican bakers. The tortillas bake up thick and are a good substitute for bread with a calabacitas or posole stew.

MAKES TWELVE 4-INCH TORTILLAS

2 cups unbleached all-purpose flour or bread flour
1 ½ cups blue corn *masa harina para tortillas* or *harinilla*
¼ cup whole wheat pastry flour
¼ cup amaranth flour or mesquite flour (see page 35)
4 teaspoons baking powder
½ teaspoon salt
1½ cups warm water
¼ cup (½ stick) cold butter, cut into pieces

1] In a medium mixing bowl using your hands or a wooden spoon or in the bowl of a heavy-duty electric mixer fitted with the paddle attachment, combine the unbleached flour, the blue cornmeal, the whole wheat and amaranth flours, baking powder, and salt. Cut in the butter until crumbly, using a fork or pastry blender if making by hand. Gradually add the hot water to the flour mixture, stirring just until the dough sticks together, clears the sides of the bowl, and a soft firm ball is formed, adding a tablespoon of water at a time if the dough seems too dry. Cover the dough with plastic wrap and let rest for 45 minutes.

2] To shape the tortillas, divide the dough into 12 equal portions. Shape each into a ball and place on a baking sheet or marble slab. Drape each ball around your forefinger, making a depression on the underside, which makes a mushroom shape and creates an air bubble to help it roll out into an even round. On a very lightly floured work surface, flatten the ball with your palm. (The flattened balls can rest on a greased baking sheet, covered tightly, for 30 minutes longer, if necessary.) Place one of the portions of the dough between 2 pieces of plastic wrap or wax paper. Press in a tortilla press, turning at regular intervals, until the desired thickness. Or roll out with a rolling pin to a 4-inch round, ¼ inch thick. Stack between layers of plastic wrap to prevent drying out while pressing out the remaining dough. Bake as soon as possible.

3] To bake the tortillas, heat a large ungreased heavy cast-iron skillet or *comal* over medium-high heat until a drop of water dances across the surface. Place the tortillas, one at a time, in the pan, and bake for about 2½ minutes. When the dough looks dry and brown spots are formed, turn over to the other side and bake for 2 to 3 minutes. Keep flipping back and forth until the tortilla is soft, not crisp; it will puff up to ½ inch thick. It is very easy to overbake, so pay close attention to the timing. Remove each tortilla to a clean towel. Cover until serving.

REGIONAL NATIVE AMERICAN BREADS: SPIRIT OF THE HEARTH

THE HORNO

The *horno,* a beehive-shaped outdoor adobe oven, arrived with the first Spanish settlers. It utilizes a construction pattern fused with local materials and the knowledge of the Native craftspeople. The simple sun-baked igloo-like *horno* on a platform still functions in pueblo and rural Spanish communities. The structures are protected historical landmarks. Built of adobe bricks (also an art learned from the Spanish) and flagstone, the old ovens needed to be rebuilt every few years, since the harsh climatic conditions tend to wear away at the mud. Modern ovens contain some cement to stabilize the structure and cracks are routinely replastered to seal in the heat.

There are three sizes of *hornos:* the Papa, the Mama, and the Baby. A Papa might be eight feet square and four feet high, with a thick dome. Often the Papa will actually be two or three connecting ovens: Up to four dozen loaves of bread can be baked in each oven at one time for a village. The opening might have a wooden door or might be blocked with a sheet of metal or even a wet flour sack. The Mama is considerably smaller, compact and moveable, accommodating two loaves at a time. This oven is placed in an indoor open fireplace, using the chimney as the smoke hole. The Baby is only a foot high and is used as a home incense burner. Backyard home *hornos* are usually about two to three feet wide, with the oven opening about one foot, easily baking two to four loaves of bread at a time.

After the bread is finished, other foods, such as whole winter squashes, roast meat and game, empanadas, panocha pudding, and *capirotada,* are baked in the declining heat. Fresh chiles are roasted as are unhusked corn cobs, which will be husked, sundried, and shelled to make chicos.

Myrtle Stedman, resident New Mexican artist and contemporary of Georgia O'Keefe and Mable Dodge Luhan, wrote an article for the August 1969 issue of *New Mexico* magazine chronicling her day helping to build a family oven at the Tesuque Pueblo. It was the first piece of its type to appear in print, reflecting the "back to earth" movement that was sweeping the Southwest at the time. Stedman's work broke new ground as a guide back to the old ways. She later revised the textbook on traditional northern New Mexico adobe architecture for the University of New Mexico, including chapters outlining how to make and lay adobe bricks and build the traditional outdoor *horno. Adobe Architecture* (Sunstone Press, 1987), still in print, is a standard reference on the subject.

Indian Adobe Oven Bread from the Santa Clara Pueblo
This is a bread that sings of the strong sun and warm earth. After building an adobe oven, comes learning how to heat and bake in it. Each oven has its own idiosyncrasies, but basic rules apply. The instinctual sense of timing needed to coordinate the heat of the fire and the baking itself is acquired by practice. A seasoned Native baker may have up to fifty years experience with this baking style, rising at dawn to light the fire and prepare the dough to bake enough loaves to feed the crowds assembled for a religious ceremony. Indian yeast bread often starts with a sponge made the afternoon before it is baked, though this recipe does not.

At least a cord of firewood and plenty of small kindling are collected; juniper, cedar, and piñon are Southwestern favorites. Jacquie likes almond or oak wood; Stedman liked fruitwood; others use aspen. On baking day, the horno *is cleaned by wiping it out with a damp cloth hung on the end of a broom handle. The wood fire is built early in the morning and let die down to white coals. This takes 4 to 5 hours.*

Often there is a sign advertising Fresh Homemade Bread For Sale at the different pueblos; it's worth a stop. South of Albuquerque, the Isleta Pueblo bakers are renowned; their loaves are baked in the ancient community ovens and sold daily.

MAKES TWENTY-FIVE 1-POUND ROUND LOAVES

About 10 cups warm water
4 envelopes active dry yeast
1 cup sugar
2 pounds lard, melted
3 tablespoons salt
1 sack (25 pounds) bleached all-purpose flour

To prepare the bread, 4 cups of the warm water are poured into a large washtub. The yeast and half of the sugar are sprinkled over it, and it is left to stand until the yeast comes to a bubble. The remaining sugar, the lard, salt, and remaining 6 cups warm water are added. Stirring constantly, enough flour is added to make a soft dough. This takes the entire sack of flour. The dough is kneaded well for at least 30 minutes. Then it is formed into a smooth round mass, the top brushed with some extra melted lard, and the bread is covered with damp towels. It is left to rise until double in bulk, 2 to 3 hours.

The dough is punched down and kneaded again for at least 10 minutes. It is divided into 25 portions, shaped into round loaves, and placed on greased pie plates. It is covered and left to rise again until double in bulk, 1 to 2 hours.

The temperature of the oven is tested by tossing a crumpled sheet of newspaper or a handful of oatmeal onto the floor. If they burn up or blacken quickly, the oven is still too hot and needs to be swabbed with water. At the right medium-high temperature, the newspaper browns gently and looks like golden-brown toast. Some bakers "bare arm" it by holding their hand and arm in the hot oven while counting to 40.

A 5-foot steel pole, garden hoe, or broom handle with a clean old towel or T-shirt soaked in water wrapped around the end is used to swab out some of the ashes. The hot ashes and coals that are cleaned out are piled into a small heap outside the oven.

Using a long-handled paddle, loaves are arranged close together on the oven floor, leaving the door open only if necessary to let the temperature drop. Otherwise, the door is closed, and the smoke flue plugged with a rock wrapped in a wet cloth to drive the heat down to the oven floor. A wet sack is placed over the door of the oven and secured there with a stick while the loaves are baking. After 1 to 1½ hours, the baked breads are removed from the oven with the wooden paddle.

INDIAN ADOBE OVEN BREAD
(Pueblo)

Baking yeasted wheat loaves in outdoor beehive ovens was taught to the Rio Grande Pueblos by the first Franciscan missionaries. The bread emerges from the wood-fired horno crisp crusted and delicate in flavor in the fashion of a good European peasant loaf. Loaves may be shaped into smooth rounds or rounds with snipped edges and with a small flower of dough known as siki 'nä on top. Some loaves are made into rings of small balls or into two, four, or six sections; others are formed into paw shapes divided into three fat fingers called mandi, or folded half-moons called pân. A special small loaf is made with a center hole so it can be threaded with yucca twine for carrying during dances. Traditional recipes call for a twenty-five- or fifty-pound bag of white flour; homemade lard, once a household staple, or solid vegetable shortening, such as Crisco; and a very small amount of yeast. The dough is often left to stand overnight at a cool temperature to develop a good flavor and texture. A twenty-five pound bag of flour would yield about twenty-five large loaves, but this recipe is for more manageable quantities.

MAKES 2 SMALL OR 1 LARGE ROUND LOAF

4 to 4½ cups unbleached all-purpose flour
   or bread flour
1 tablespoon sugar
2 teaspoons active dry yeast
1 teaspoon salt
1½ cups hot water (120°F.)
2 tablespoons unsalted butter, shortening, or lard,
   at room temperature

1] In a large bowl with a whisk or in the bowl of a heavy-duty electric mixer fitted with the paddle attachment, combine 1½ cups of the flour, the sugar, yeast, salt, and hot water. Beat on medium speed until smooth, about 1 minute. Add the butter and the remaining flour, ½ cup at a time, and mix on low speed until a soft shaggy dough that just clears the sides of the bowl forms, switching to a wooden spoon when necessary if making by hand.

2] Turn the dough out onto a lightly floured work surface and knead until smooth and springy, 1 to 2 minutes for a machine-mixed dough and 3 to 5 minutes for a hand-mixed dough, dusting with flour only 1 tablespoon at a time, just enough as needed to prevent sticking. Place in a greased deep container, turn once to coat the top, and cover with plastic wrap. Let rise at room temperature until double in bulk, 2 to 3 hours.

3] Grease or line a baking sheet with parchment paper or grease or line two 9-inch pie plates. Turn the dough out onto a lightly floured work surface and divide into 2 equal portions. Shape into 2 tight rounds and place on the baking sheet or pie plates. Or leave intact and shape into 1 tight round and place on the baking sheet.

4] Cover with a clean towel or piece of plastic wrap, and let the loaves rest at room temperature until puffy, about 45 minutes.

5] About 20 minutes before baking, preheat the oven to 450°F., with a baking stone on the lowest and top oven racks, if desired.

6] Reduce the heat to 400°F. Bake the loaves in the center of the oven or on the lower stone for 35 to 40 minutes, until the loaves are golden brown and sound hollow when tapped with your finger. Remove from the baking sheet and cool on racks. You may also use La Cloche (see page 146). Loaves are best slightly warm or at room temperature the day they are baked.

VARIATIONS

Paw Shape: Flatten each portion with a rolling pin into a thick round about 8 inches in diameter. Place each round on the baking sheet or pie plate, and press to flatten slightly. Lightly brush half the dough surface on each round with water. Fold in half over the wet surface, bringing the top section within ½ inch of the bottom edge. With a sharp knife, cut the rounded edge twice about half of the way through the loaf to open it into 3 fat sections. Spread each cut about 1 inch apart to form the bear paw shape. Brush the top with melted butter. Continue with Steps 4, 5, and 6.

Ring: Divide the dough into 12 equal portions. Roll each piece of the dough into a ball and arrange five of the balls ½ inch apart in a circle on the baking sheet or pie plate. Set 1 ball in the center. Make a second loaf in the same manner. Continue with Steps 4, 5, and 6.

Divided loaf: Divide the dough into 2 sections and form each into an oval. Dip the flat edge of the side of your outstretched hand in some flour, and then press into the center of each loaf lengthwise to define a separation. Continue with Steps 4, 5, and 6.

TAOS SUN BREAD
(Pueblo)

The sun is central in Southwest Native cosmology, since it makes life possible. Upon awakening at dawn, a Pueblo male thanks the sun for rising by tossing a pinch of white cornmeal toward the east. This bread is formed into a corona sunburst crescent, a sculpted tribute to the rising sun, a form also known as the bear paw. This shape is commonly made in the Rio Grande pueblos.

MAKES 2 LOAVES

2 cups water
½ cup white or yellow cornmeal, fine- or
    medium-grind
⅓ cup honey
3 tablespoons corn oil or melted lard
1 tablespoon (1 package) active dry yeast
Pinch of light brown sugar or large drop of honey
¼ cup warm water (105° to 115°F.)
2 teaspoons salt
½ cup dried buttermilk powder
½ cup whole wheat pastry flour
3¾ to 4¼ cups unbleached all-purpose flour or
    bread flour

1] In a medium saucepan, bring the 2 cups of water to a boil. Stirring constantly with a whisk (Native cooks used stir sticks), pour in the cornmeal in a steady stream. Reduce heat to a simmer and cook, stirring constantly, for 5 minutes, or to a thick and smooth soft porridge. Stir in the honey and oil. Scrape into a large mixing bowl or the bowl of a heavy-duty electric mixer. Set aside to cool 20 minutes.

2] Meanwhile, in a small bowl, sprinkle the yeast and the brown sugar over the warm water. Stir until dissolved. Let stand until foamy, about 10 minutes.

3] Using a whisk or the paddle attachment of the mixer, add the salt, buttermilk powder, and whole wheat flour to the cornmeal mixture. Beat hard on medium speed until combined, about 1 minute. Add the yeast mixture and 1 cup of the unbleached flour, beating on medium speed for 1 minute more. Add the rest of the unbleached flour, H cup at a time, mixing on low speed until a soft shaggy dough that just clears the sides of the bowl forms, switching to a wooden spoon when necessary if making by hand.

4] Turn out the dough onto a lightly floured work surface and knead until smooth and elastic, 1 to 2 minutes for a machine-mixed dough and 3 to 5 minutes for a hand-mixed dough, dusting with flour only 1 tablespoon at a time, just enough as needed to prevent sticking. The dough will retain a nubby, tacky quality, yet be quite soft. Place in a greased deep container, turn once to coat the top, and cover with plastic wrap. Let rise at room temperature until double in bulk, 1 to 1H hours.

5] Grease or line a baking sheet with parchment paper. Turn out the dough onto a work surface sprinkled heavily with cornmeal and divide into 2 equal portions. Form each portion into a round ball with just a few kneads and roll or pat out to a round about 10 inches in diameter and about 1 inch thick. Press down with the back of a knife to make a crease about 1 inch off center. Fold the smaller half over the larger. Using a sharp knife, make two 3-inch deep cuts along the curved edge of the dough; the loaf will appear divided into thirds. Carefully transfer both loaves onto the prepared baking sheet, spacing them at least 3 inches apart and arranging the loaf so that the cut edges fan apart slightly. Cover loosely with plastic wrap and let rise at room temperature until double in bulk, about 45 minutes.

6] About 20 minutes before baking, preheat the oven to 450°F., with a baking stone on the lowest oven rack, if desired.

7] Reduce the oven heat to 400°F. Bake the loaves in the center of the oven or on the lower hot stone for 15 minutes. Reduce the oven heat again, this time to 350°F., and bake for 25 to 30 minutes more, until the loaf is crusty and golden brown and sounds hollow when tapped with your finger. Remove bread to a rack to cool completely before slicing. Loaves are best slightly warm or at room temperature the day they are baked.

ZUNI SUNFLOWER WHEAT BREAD

(Pueblo)

The sunflower is sacred to the Southwest Natives, a symbol linked to the sun and its influence over food plant growth. Fresh sunflower blossoms marked Apache prayers for a good harvest. Sunflower seeds were harvested from the heads of dried sunflowers and left to dry on the roof for winter food storage. Ground seeds and nuts are an integral part of Native breads.

MAKES 2 ROUND LOAVES

1½ tablespoons (1½ packages) active dry yeast
¼ cup (packed) light brown sugar
1¼ cups warm water (105° to 115°F.)
2¼ cups whole raw sunflower seeds
2¼ cups whole wheat flour
1 cup warm evaporated milk or evaporated
   goat's milk (105° to 115°F.)
¼ cup vegetable oil or ¼ cup (½ stick) unsalted
   butter, melted
2½ teaspoons salt
3 to 3½ cups unbleached all-purpose flour
   or bread flour

1] In a small bowl, sprinkle the yeast and a pinch of the brown sugar over ½ cup of the warm water. Stir until dissolved. Let stand until foamy, about 10 minutes.

2] Meanwhile, in a food processor, combine 1½ cups of the sunflower seeds and the whole wheat flour and process to the consistency of coarse meal. Set aside.

3] In a large bowl with a whisk or in the bowl of a heavy-duty electric mixer fitted with the paddle attachment, combine the remaining ¾ cup warm water and remaining brown sugar, the milk, oil, salt, the remaining ¾ cup whole sunflower seeds, and 1 cup of the unbleached flour. Beat

on medium speed until smooth, about 1 minute. Add the yeast and seed-flour mixture. Beat 1 minute more. Add the unbleached flour, ½ cup at a time, mixing on low speed until a soft shaggy dough that just clears the sides of the bowl forms, switching to a wooden spoon when necessary if making by hand.

4] Turn out the dough onto a lightly floured work surface and knead until soft and springy, 1 to 2 minutes for a machine-mixed dough and 3 to 5 minutes for a hand-mixed dough, dusting with flour only 1 tablespoon at a time, just enough as needed to prevent sticking. Do not add more flour than required, or the dough will get stiff and the bread will bake up too dry. Place in a greased deep container, turn once to coat the top, and cover with plastic wrap. Let rise at room temperature until double in bulk, 1½ to 2 hours.

5] Grease or line a baking sheet with parchment paper. Turn out the dough onto a clean work surface and divide into 2 equal portions. Form each portion into a tight round. Place on the baking sheet, dust the tops with flour, and cover loosely with plastic wrap. Let rise at room temperature until double in bulk, about 50 minutes.

6] About 20 minutes before baking, preheat the oven to 450°F., with a baking stone on the lowest oven rack, if desired.

7] Using a sharp knife, slash the surface of each loaf decoratively, no more than ¼ inch deep. Reduce the oven heat to 375°F. Bake the loaves in the center of the oven or on the hot stone for 35 to 40 minutes, or until the loaves are golden brown and sound hollow when tapped with your finger. Remove from the baking sheet and cool on racks.

TAOS PUMPKIN BREAD
(Pueblo)

This bread originally appeared in my first book, Bread, *without the toasted cornmeal. A crusty, sienna-colored Southwest bread with an irresistible earthy flavor, it is likely to appear for the fall harvest celebrations. Consider using one of the heirloom squash varieties, such as the Acoma Pumpkin with its blue fruit, or Calabaza Mexicana, the long-neck pumpkin.*

MAKES 2 ROUND LOAVES

1½ cups warm water (105° to 115°F.)

1 tablespoon (1 package) active dry yeast

½ cup (packed) light brown sugar or 1 cone *piloncillo,* crumbled

2 large eggs

1 cup pumpkin puree, canned or homemade (page 141)

1 tablespoon salt

½ cup fine-grind yellow or white cornmeal, toasted, or *masa harina para tortillas,* toasted

5½ to 6 cups unbleached all-purpose flour or bread flour

3 tablespoons *each* yellow cornmeal and unbleached flour, mixed, for sprinkling

1] Pour ½ cup of the warm water into a small bowl or 1-cup liquid measuring cup. Sprinkle the yeast and a pinch of the sugar over the surface of the water. Stir to dissolve and let stand at room temperature until foamy, about 10 minutes.

2] In a large bowl using a whisk or in the bowl of a heavy-duty electric mixer fitted with the paddle attachment, combine the eggs and pumpkin puree. Add the remaining water and brown sugar, the salt, cornmeal, and 2 cups of the flour. Beat on medium speed until smooth, about 1 minute. Add the yeast mixture and beat vigorously for 1 minute more.

Add the remaining flour, ½ cup at a time, mixing on low speed until a soft shaggy dough that just clears the sides of the bowl forms, switching to a wooden spoon when necessary if making by hand.

3] Turn the dough out onto a lightly floured work surface and knead to create a soft, smooth, and elastic dough, 1 to 2 minutes for a machine-mixed dough and 3 to 5 minutes for a hand-mixed dough, adding flour only 1 tablespoon at a time, just enough as needed to prevent sticking. Add enough of the remaining flour for the dough to hold its own shape. Place in a greased deep container, turn once to coat the top, and cover with plastic wrap. Let rise at room temperature until double in bulk, 1 to 1½ hours.

4] Line a baking sheet or wooden peel with parchment paper and sprinkle with the combination of cornmeal and flour. Gently deflate the dough and turn it out onto a lightly floured surface. Divide the dough into 2 equal portions. Form into 2 round loaves and place on the baking sheet. Cover loosely with plastic wrap and let rise for 30 minutes, or until double in bulk.

5] About 20 minutes before baking, preheat the oven to 450°F., using a baking stone set in the lower third of the oven, if desired. Dust the tops of loaves with flour.

6] Using a serrated knife, slash loaves decoratively, no deeper than ¼ inch. Slide the loaves with the layer of parchment, if used, directly onto the stone (the parchment is easily removed later) in the oven, or place the baking sheet on the stone. Immediately reduce the oven temperature to 375°F., and bake for 45 to 55 minutes, or until loaves are lightly browned and sound hollow when tapped with your finger. Remove the parchment and cool on racks before serving.

WHITE SAGE BREAD

(Pueblo)

*Every collection of Native Southwest breads recipes includes one
for a fresh cheese-based dough flavored with the wild white sage
that grows prolifically in the area. In the absence of wild white
sage, cultivated varieties can be substituted perfectly.*

MAKES 2 SMALL ROUND LOAVES

1¼ cups warm water (105° TO 115°F.)
1 tablespoon (1 package) active dry yeast
3 tablespoons sugar or honey
5 to 5¼ cups unbleached all-purpose flour
¼ cup vegetable or sunflower oil
2 tablespoons chopped fresh wild white sage leaves
    or cultivated sage leaves, or 1 tablespoon dried sage
2 teaspoons salt
2 large eggs
1¼ cups small-curd cottage cheese
Egg Glaze (page 127)
½ cup crushed toasted pine nuts or 2 tablespoons
    coarse salt, for sprinkling

1] Pour the warm water into a small bowl or 1-cup liquid
measuring cup. Sprinkle the yeast and the sugar over the
surface of the water. Stir to dissolve and add 2 cups of the
flour. Beat hard with a whisk until creamy and well combined, about 15 strokes. Cover loosely with plastic wrap
and let stand at room temperature until bubbly, about
1 hour.

2] In a large bowl using a whisk or in the bowl of a heavy-
duty electric mixer fitted with the paddle attachment,
combine the sponge and 1 cup of the flour, the oil, sage,
salt, eggs, and cottage cheese. Beat on medium speed until
creamy, about 1 minute. Add the remaining flour, ½ cup
at a time, beating on low speed until a soft shaggy dough
that just clears the sides of the bowl forms, switching to
a wooden spoon when necessary if making by hand.

3] Turn the dough out onto a lightly floured work surface
and knead until soft and springy, 1 to 2 minutes for a
machine-mixed dough and 2 to 4 minutes for a hand-
mixed dough, dusting with flour only 1 tablespoon at a
time, just enough as needed to prevent sticking. The dough
will be delicate, smooth, and lightly springy to the touch,
but not dry, yet able to hold its shape. Place the dough in a
greased deep container, turn once to coat the top, and cover
with plastic wrap. Let rise at room temperature until just
double in bulk, 1 to 1¼ hours. Do not let the dough rise
more than double at this point or it will collapse in the
oven.

4] Grease or line a baking sheet with parchment paper.
Turn out the dough onto a clean work surface and divide
into 2 equal portions. Form each portion into a tight
round. Place on the baking sheet, dust the tops with flour,
and cover loosely with plastic wrap. Let rise at room temperature until double in bulk, about 50 minutes.

5] About 20 minutes before baking, preheat the oven
to 350°F., with a baking stone on the lowest oven rack,
if desired.

6] Using a sharp knife, slash the surface of each loaf with
an X, no more than ¼ inch deep. Brush the tops with the
glaze, and sprinkle with the crushed pine nuts or sprinkle
with coarse salt, as desired. Bake the loaves in the center
of the oven or on the hot stone for 30 to 35 minutes, or
until the loaves are golden brown and sound hollow when
tapped with your finger. Remove from the baking sheet
and cool on racks.

MASA BREAD

(Pueblo)

Masa harina para tortillas *is used to prepare this bread. Mexican bakers prefer white cornmeal, but Native bakers use yellow and blue cornmeals well.*

MAKES 2 SMALL ROUND LOAVES

3¾ to 4¼ cups unbleached all-purpose flour
1¼ cups white, yellow, or blue *masa harina para tortillas*
1 tablespoon (1 package) active dry yeast
3 tablespoons (packed) dark brown sugar or
  ½ cone *piloncillo,* crumbled
2 teaspoons salt
2 cups hot water (120°F.)
Cornmeal, for sprinkling
2 tablespoons corn oil, for brushing

1] In a large bowl using a whisk or in the bowl of a heavy-duty electric mixer fitted with the paddle attachment, combine 1 cup of the unbleached flour, the cornmeal, yeast, sugar, and salt. Add the hot water and beat on medium speed until smooth, about 1 minute. Add the remaining flour, ½ cup at a time, mixing on low speed until a soft shaggy dough that just clears the sides of the bowl forms, switching to a wooden spoon when necessary if making by hand.

2] Turn the dough out onto a lightly floured work surface and knead until soft and springy, 1 to 2 minutes for a machine-mixed dough and 3 to 5 minutes for a hand-mixed dough, dusting with flour only 1 tablespoon at a time, just enough as needed to prevent sticking. The dough will be smooth and springy, but not dry. Place in a greased deep container, turn once to coat the top, and cover with plastic wrap. Let rise at room temperature until double in bulk, 1 to 1½ hours.

3] Turn the dough out onto a lightly floured work surface to deflate. Line a baking sheet with parchment or grease two 9-inch cake pans and sprinkle them with cornmeal. Without working the dough further, divide it into 2 equal portions. Form into 2 tight round loaves. Place the loaves on the baking sheet at least 4 inches apart to allow for expansion. Brush the tops with the corn oil, to keep the surface soft. Cover loosely with plastic wrap and let rise at room temperature until the dough is fully double in bulk, about 45 minutes.

4] About 20 minutes before baking, preheat the oven to 375°F.

5] Brush the tops again with the corn oil. Place the pans on the center rack of the oven and bake for 30 to 35 minutes, or until the loaves are golden brown and sound hollow when tapped with your finger. Remove the loaves from the pans immediately to a cooling rack. Loaves are best served warm or at room temperature the day they are baked.

INDIAN FRUIT TURNOVERS
(Pueblo)

Baked fruit-filled turnovers are a must for Christmas celebrations. The dried fruit and honey filling can be varied to your taste by the choice of fruit. The pumpkin filling is a traditional one. Sweet small pumpkins are cut in half and hung to dry in the sun on posts. The dried pumpkin is reconstituted like dried fruit. Many turnovers are made with lard biscuit doughs, but this is a Pueblo yeast dough. These are served at the Indian Pueblo Cultural Center in Albuquerque for all feasts. If you like, drizzle with a Powdered Sugar Glaze (page 127), as a finishing touch.

MAKES 18 TURNOVERS

4 teaspoons active dry yeast
1 teaspoon sugar
¼ cup warm water (105° TO 115°F.)
¾ cup warm milk (105° TO 115°F.)
¼ cup fine-grind yellow cornmeal
3¼ to 3½ cups unbleached all-purpose flour
3 tablespoons sugar
½ teaspoon salt
1 large egg
½ cup (1 stick) unsalted butter, at room temperature, cut into pieces
Fruit Honey Filling *(recipe follows)*
Sweet Pumpkin Filling *(recipe follows)*

1] In a medium bowl or in the bowl of a heavy-duty electric mixer fitted with the paddle attachment, sprinkle the yeast and sugar over the warm water. Stir to dissolve and let stand until bubbly, about 10 minutes. Add the milk, cornmeal, ½ cup of the flour, the sugar, salt, and egg. Beat with a whisk or on medium speed until smooth. Gradually add 1½ cups more of the flour until a soft dough is formed. Add the butter, 1 tablespoon at a time, and beat until incorporated. Add the remaining flour, ½ cup at a time and heat

on low speed, until a soft shaggy dough that just clears the sides of the bowl forms, switching to a wooden spoon when necessary if making by hand. The dough should be moist, yet just hold together when patted into a round. Chill in plastic wrap for at least 1 hour or up to 1 day. Reserve any extra flour.

2] Grease or line two 10-by-15-inch baking sheets with parchment paper. Divide the pastry into 2 equal portions. On a lightly floured work surface, roll out 1 pastry portion to a 12-inch square about ¼ inch thick. Keep the second portion covered. Using a sharp knife or pastry wheel, cut into 4-inch squares. Place 2 tablespoons of the fruit filling on the bottom half of a pastry square and fold over to make a triangle. Crimp the edges with the tines of a fork to seal. Place the pastries on a baking sheet, 1 inch apart. Repeat with the second portion filling each square with prepared filling. Place on the second baking sheet. Brush the tops with oil. Let stand, uncovered, for 20 minutes at room temperature, or until puffy.

3] Meanwhile, preheat the oven to 400°F.

4] Bake, one pan at a time, in the center of the oven, 15 to 18 minutes, or until the surface is golden brown and dry to the touch. (Refrigerate the other baking sheet until ready to bake if the dough is rising fast.) Remove from the pan with a metal spatula to a rack to cool.

FRUIT HONEY FILLING
Makes enough for 18 turnovers

8 ounces dried fruit, such as dried apples,
    apricots, peaches, or prunes
⅔ cup honey

In a large saucepan, combine the dried fruit and water. Bring to a boil, reduce the heat, and simmer, uncovered, until soft, about 30 minutes. Mash the fruit, or puree with an immersion blender or food processor. Add the honey. Cool to room temperature before using. Filling makes enough for one batch of turnovers. May be made ahead and refrigerated overnight. (Filling may be kept, covered, for up to 1 week in the refrigerator.)

SWEET PUMPKIN FILLING
Makes enough for 18 turnovers

1½ cups pumpkin puree, canned or homemade
    (page 141)
½ cup (packed) light brown sugar
⅓ cup honey
1 teaspoon ground cinnamon
Pinch of ground allspice
Pinch of ground ginger
1 teaspoon grated orange zest

Combine the pumpkin, honey, spices, and zest in a small saucepan. Cook over medium heat, uncovered, until thick, about 15 minutes. Cool to room temperature before using. Filling makes enough for one batch of turnovers. May be made ahead and refrigerated overnight. (Filling may be kept, covered for up to 1 week in the refrigerator.)

INDIAN FRY BREAD
(Navajo)

Navajo Dah di Niel Hyash is a common sight at pow-wows, rodeos, and state fairs. Fry Bread is another story in frugal culinary creativity, having been taught to the interned Navajos at Fort Sumner by the U.S. Army wives. The Navajos had never used wheat flour or baking powder to make dough before being issued monthly rations. The bread is now standard fare for many other Indian nations. It is often filled with picadillo.

Fry bread dough is flattened by hand, which takes practice. Novice bakers usually use a rolling pin and cut the dough into squares or rounds. Some bakers poke a small hole in the middle, left over from the days of flipping it with a long stick. Make certain the cooking oil is hot enough, or the fry breads will be doughy, undercooked, and oily. Remember to cool the fry breads with the bubble side (the one that cooks first) up, so that "people won't go hungry, but will get full from your fry bread," as the Navajo say.

I have been advised that KC baking powder (available on the reservations), Bluebird flour from Cortez, Colorado, Army-issue dried milk, and Crisco solid shortening for frying are the ingredients that give the most traditional flavor. Coltsfoot ashes (Tussilago) appear in early recipes as a salty addition, as do ground sunflower seeds. When this dough is baked on a griddle, it is known as Tortilla Bread.

MAKES 16 TO 20 FRY BREADS

4 cups unbleached all-purpose flour
½ cup nonfat dry milk
1½ tablespoons baking powder
1 teaspoon salt
4 tablespoons vegetable shortening or lard
1½ cups very hot water
Flour or cornmeal, for dusting
2 quarts vegetable oil, for deep frying
Picadillo (recipe follows), for serving (optional)

1] In a mixing bowl or in the bowl of a heavy-duty electric mixer fitted with the paddle attachment, combine the flour, dry milk, baking powder and salt. Cut in the shortening or lard until crumbly using a knife or a pastry blender if making by hand.

2] Add the water and mix well, using a fork if mixing by hand, until the dough comes together into a ball. Knead briefly in the bowl, no more than 10 times, until a soft and smooth, but not sticky, ball forms. Cover loosely with plastic wrap and let the dough rest at room temperature for at least 30 minutes.

3] On a flour- or cornmeal-dusted work surface, pull off small knobs of dough 2 to 3 inches in diameter to make 16 to 20 pieces. Working with 1 piece at a time (leave the other dough pieces covered with a damp towel), overlap the outer edge toward the center ¼ inch, then roll the knob out into a thin circle with a rolling pin. Cover with plastic wrap and repeat with the remaining pieces. Let rest for about 20 minutes.

4] Heat 2 inches of oil in a Dutch oven, wok, heavy kettle, or deep-fat fryer to 380°F. Working in batches, drop the dough, one piece at a time, into the hot oil, tapping and

pushing the pieces gently with tongs to keep them immersed until they bubble up and become golden and crisp. Halfway through the cooking of the first side, gently turn the dough over to cook evenly. Cook for about 2 minutes total on each side, piercing the edge with a fork when turning over. Remove with a slotted spoon and drain, one on top of the other, bubble side up, on paper towels or clean brown paper bags. Breads may also be kept warm in a 200°F. oven. Serve with picadillo, if desired.

VARIATION

Honey Indian Fry Bread: Add ¼ cup desert honey to the hot water in Step 2. Continue to mix, shape, and fry as for Indian Fry Bread.

PICADILLO

Makes enough for 8 fry breads

> 1 pound ground meat, such as beef, lamb, pork, venison, duck, or buffalo
> 1 clove garlic, minced
> 2 large shallots, chopped
> 1 to 2 tablespoons vegetable oil
> 1 tablespoon red wine vinegar
> 1 cup chopped tomatoes and juice, fresh or canned
> 1 small apple, peeled, cored, and chopped
> 1 teaspoon salt
> ½ teaspoon ground cinnamon
> ½ teaspoon ground cumin
> ¼ cup dried currants or diced candied pumpkin
> ¼ cup pine nuts

In a heavy large skillet over medium heat, sauté the ground meat, garlic, and shallots in oil until browned. Add the vinegar, tomatoes, apple, salt, and spices. Simmer, uncovered, over medium-low heat, until all the liquid is evaporated. Stir in the currants and pine nuts. Serve hot. Can be refrigerated overnight and reheated.

KNEELDOWN BREAD
(Navajo)

Also known as Navajo tamales, Kneeldown Bread is baked in a corn husk. It used to be made in bulk after the corn harvest and stored over the winter like a hard cracker. One old recipe reads as follows: "Scrape the kernels from fresh corn cobs and grind on a metate until mushy. Wrap in several layers of corn husks. Place in the ashes of a wood fire and cover with fresh corn husks or leaves to seal in the heat and steam. Cover with a layer of moist dirt, then a layer of hot coals. Stoke a small fire over all the layers and bake the breads about 1 hour. Remove the packets from the ash pit, peel off the husks, and eat hot." Modern recipes utilize a hand grinder or food processor and an indoor oven as well as an underground outdoor fire. Kneeldown Bread is sometimes sold by vendors at flea markets. Cold bread is commonly eaten dunked in hot coffee.

MAKES 10 BREADS

10 ears fresh corn
3 tablespoons lard
1⅓ cups water
Salt to taste

1] Husk the corn, reserving the husks for wrapping. Using a sharp knife, cut the kernels off the cob. Scrape down the cob with the dull side of the blade to release the corn milk. In a food processor, grind the kernels to a mush. Add the lard, water, and salt, and process just enough to make a paste.

2] Divide the mixture into 10 equal portions. To fill the husks, lay out the husk so that the natural curl faces up to enclose the filling. Spoon the filling lengthwise into the center of the husk. Using strips of husks, tie both ends to enclose the filling. Gently bend the bread in half to tie the two ends together. Wrap each bread in aluminum foil and place on a baking sheet or in a roasting pan.

3] Preheat the oven to 350°F.

4] Place the pan in the center of the oven and bake for 1 hour, or until breads are firm to the touch. Serve hot. Store in the refrigerator up to 5 days.

PUBERTY CORN CAKE
(Navajo)

This beautiful tribal bread is still made in the traditional manner during reservation ceremonies to honor a young woman, as well as for other special family occasions. I had heard stories from participants of how this ash bread was prepared and shared, and so I was pleased to find written directions by Carolyn Niethammer in her American Indian Food and Lore (Macmillian, 1974). Ash breads like this were standard fare for all the nomadic tribes, usually small three-inch round cakes fashioned from a stiff dough and placed in a pit with hot embers, then covered with more ashes and hot coals. The cake is often as much as five feet across and eight inches thick. It is baked overnight while the family sings and dances. The first piece is cut from the center to be shared among the lead singers. Sprouted oat flour is sometimes used instead of panocha (sprouted wheat) flour. Today, most bakers pour the batter into a foil-lined and foil-topped baking pan and bake the cake slowly in a 200°F. oven until firm.

MAKES 1 VERY LARGE ROUND BREAD

2 pounds fine-grind yellow or white cornmeal,
    preferably stone-ground
1 cup panocha flour
1 pound dark raisins
6 cups boiling water
1½ to 2 pounds fresh or dried corn husks,
    soaked for 2 hours in water
Cornmeal, for sprinkling

1] Dig a hole in the ground for the fire; it must be larger than the diameter of the cake and at least 6 inches deep. Build a wood fire in the depression and let it burn until it falls to ashes and embers.

2] In a large bowl, combine the cornmeal, panocha flour, raisins, and boiling water, and stir to break up any lumps. Cool. Remove the embers and ashes to make a clean space for the bread. Line the pit with several overlapping and crisscrossed layers of wet corn husks. Pour the cornmeal mixture into the lined pit and sprinkle with cornmeal. (Native bakers bless the cake at this time by sprinkling prayer-meal from east to west, then south to north, then toward the sun). Cover with more wet corn husks and top with a thick layer of wet newspapers or cardboard. Cover completely with 3 inches of damp earth. Build another wood fire on top of the earth and keep it going for 8 hours.

3] Remove the layers of ashes, earth, newspaper, and corn husks; the cake will be solid. Remove the corn husks before placing in a basket and serve.

DESERT BREAD PUFFS
(Tohono O'odham)

These savory bread puffs are adapted from a Tohono O'odham feast day recipe recorded by Native American food and culture expert E. Barrie Kavasch.

MAKES ABOUT 20 PUFFS

1½ cups bleached or unbleached all-purpose flour
½ cup tepary bean flour (see page 142) or
  amaranth flour
1½ tablespoons baking powder
¼ teaspoon salt
Pinch of chili powder
Pinch of ground cumin or chopped fresh
  oregano leaves
½ cup (packed) fresh cilantro, minced
2 green onions, minced
1 small green chile, roasted, peeled, seeded, and diced
  (page 137)
1 cup low-fat milk
4 cups vegetable oil, for frying

1] In a medium mixing bowl, combine the dry ingredients, spices, herbs, green onions, and chile. Make a well in the center and pour in the milk. Stir with a wooden spoon until a sticky dough is formed.

2] Heat 1 inch of oil in a Dutch oven or cast-iron frying pan to 380°F. Working in batches, drop the batter by the heaping tablespoonful into the hot oil, taking care that they do not touch each other. Fry until golden, turning as necessary. Remove with a slotted spoon and drain on paper towels or clean brown paper bags. Bread puffs may be kept warm in a 200°F. oven.

TRADITIONAL PIKI BREAD

The batter for traditional piki is made with cold, not boiling water. A wood fire is built under the piki stone and a large wire rack or pile of paper towels is placed near it. The cold water is slowly mixed into the dough, thinning it into a crepelike batter. If the batter thickens during baking it is thinned with more cold water. When hot, the stone is rubbed with watermelon seeds, or the brain or spinal cord of a sheep, until very slick. Rerub as needed. The batter is scooped up with curved fingers and spread across the hot stone, moving from right to left and back again, until it is completely covered. When the edges dry and separate from the stone surface, the piki is peeled off and placed on the cooling rack. While the next piki is baking, the first sheet is placed on top to soften while the batter cooks under it. The two are folded up together and stacked in a basket. This continues until all of the batter is used up.

CLASSIC SPANISH AND MEXICAN BREADS: MISSIONARY WHEAT

. . . Men kept herds of goats or wild horses running around the stacks of golden wheat and oats, stacked high on round, earthen eras *[threshing grounds] until trampled to the ground. The herd was turned out and the men winnowed the grain in the wind, with their wooden forks, much the same as the Israelites used to do. The women, with their shawls wound tightly around their heads and tied in a knot in the back, came in with their gray sage brooms, swept a clean space on one end of the era, where two men stood holding between them a* criba *[sieve]. The women poured into it the straw-mixed grain from their baskets, and the men rocking the* criba *back and forth sifted the grain . . . . They filled mud* torjas *[storage silos] to the ceiling with rich grain, for these great big houses were built for abundance. In those years Taos county had become the granary of New Mexico.*
Cleofas M. Jaramillo, *Genuine New Mexico Tasty Recipes* (Ancient City Press, reprinted 1981)

Spanish and Mexican settlers created the essence of Southwest baking as we know it today—the flour tortilla, fry breads, yeast breads, and sweet breads. Much of what we know about the early Spanish kitchen has been preserved in the writings of Cleofas Jaramillo's family recipe books and accounts of daily life. She founded La Sociedad Folklórica de Santa Fe early this century.

The *cocina*, or kitchen, was the center of daily Southwest mission and family life. It offered a cooling place of respite from the hot desert sun and ever-present dust. Like the other rooms, the kitchen door and windows of the *rancho* faced a completely enclosed patio. Indoor furnishings in the *cocina* were sparse: perhaps a *trastero*, or hutchlike storage cupboard, for keeping household pottery and the *batería de cocina*, and a large weathered plank harvest table and sturdy chairs. Kitchen walls were often decorated with colorful Mexican glazed tiles reflecting the colors of the sunsets and mountains, while cool flagstone and *saltillo* tiles later replaced humble hard-packed polished dirt floors that were polished with ox-blood. Traditional black-and-white twill throw rugs, known as *jergas*, dotted the floor.

A hand-carved *bulto* figure of San Pascual Baylón, patron saint of the kitchen, would be set into the *trastero*, a niche in the wall. His sacred mission was to link the household kitchen tasks with the celestial hierarchy. The *fogon*, or molded corner fireplace, was set in where two walls join. (Later wood-burning cook stoves providing constant warmth as well as an oven and rising area for yeast doughs were installed.) The outdoor *barbacoa* pit, a table-shaped *braseros* (Spanish for hearth), or mud stove with round holes to set the earthenware pots to set in, and adobe beehive ovens were constructed outside.

Mesquite wood tortilla presses made the shaping of delicate corn tortillas a quick and easy job, but seasoned bakers can deftly pat and roll out four flour tortillas at a time. An earthenware clay *comal*, and later the round-shaped dark cast-iron tapa stove lid of a wood- or coal-burning stove, was set over the fire to bake the endless stacks of these flat breads for every meal. The hot tortillas were kept in a *chiquihuite*, a traditional woven basket designed especially for bringing the fresh tortillas to the table. All breads were made at home until the restaurant boom at the turn of the century, with the Harvey House chain and large hotels offering their own kitchen baked specialties.

If the homestead was situated on a river or stream, then there might be a small water-powered mill for grinding grain. Otherwise grain was sent to the *molino,* or flour mill, outside of town. Suspended cone-shaped hoppers made of bull hides dropped the grain onto a revolving stone that crushed the grain against a stationary stone. Stored in sacks, the wheat flour was sifted at home onto clean canvas; the first sifting yielding the *semita* (whole wheat flour), and the second, thicker cloth sieve for the fine flour used for pastries. Blue and white corn were roasted before being sent to the mill.

Until relatively recently, all food was raised at home except for some a few luxury items. Shopping was done from traveling vendors who carried goods from village to village on their burros. The protected inner courtyard was often planted with grape arbors, flowering shrubs, and herbs, olive and fruit trees. The *huerta familiar,* or kitchen garden, was part orchard, part vegetable garden, and part herb garden. Field corn, white Sonoran wheat, and oats were grown for bread and tortillas. This garden tradition is still evident in rural Native and Hispanic communities today.

BREAD OF THE DEAD

Pan de Muerto

Pan de Muerto *is a special egg bread flavored with orange and anise that is made especially for November 2, All Soul's Day, a Mexican national holiday honoring the deceased. This is a very happy loaf, despite the name. Loaves representing the souls of the deceased are taken to the cemetery to "feed the spirits." They are decorated with dough shaped into a skull, bones, and tears, often all liberally sprinkled with crunchy pink decorative sugar crystals or sesame seeds for happiness. Loaves may also be shaped into human figures, reminiscent of the ancient Aztec monos fashioned from cornmeal doughs prepared for sacrifices, or impressed with the face of a saint. Decorate your centerpiece loaf with lots of fresh yellow marigolds or* cempascúchil, *the flower of the dead.*

MAKES 2 LARGE ROUND LOAVES

Sponge
½ cup water
1 tablespoon (1 package) active dry yeast
1 tablespoon sugar
1 cup unbleached all-purpose flour or bread flour

Dough
2 tablespoons aniseed
⅓ cup water
5 large eggs
2 tablespoons orange liqueur
½ cup (1 stick) unsalted butter, melted and cooled
Grated zest of 1 large orange
½ cup sugar
2 teaspoons salt
3¼ to 3½ cups unbleached all-purpose flour
   or bread flour

Sweet Powdered Sugar Glaze
1 cup sifted powdered sugar
2 to 3 tablespoons milk, cream sherry, or orange liqueur
½ teaspoon pure vanilla extract, if using milk

1] To prepare the sponge: In a large mixing bowl or plastic container with a whisk or in the bowl of a heavy-duty electric mixer fitted with the paddle attachment, beat on low speed the ½ cup of water, yeast, sugar, and flour until smooth. Scrape down the sides and cover with plastic wrap. Let stand at room temperature until bubbly, about 1 hour. Meanwhile, in a small saucepan, combine the aniseed and ⅓ cup of water. Boil until the liquid is reduced to 3 tablespoons, about 3 minutes. Strain and discard the aniseeds. Set aside.

2] To prepare the dough: Stir down the sponge and add the eggs, orange liqueur, aniseed water, butter, orange zest, sugar, salt, and 1 cup of the flour. Beat on medium speed until creamy, about 1 minute. Continue to add the flour, ¼ cup at a time, mixing on low speed until a soft dough that just clears the sides of the bowl forms, switching to a wooden spoon as necessary if making by hand.

3] Turn out the dough onto a lightly floured work surface and knead until a soft, smooth, and springy dough forms, 1 to 2 minutes for a machine-mixed dough and 3 to 5 minutes for a hand-mixed dough, adding only 1 tablespoon flour at a time as necessary to prevent sticking. Place in a greased deep container, turn once to coat the top, and cover with plastic wrap. Let rise at room temperature until double in bulk, 1½ to 2 hours.

4] Grease or line a baking sheet with parchment paper. Turn out the dough onto the floured work surface and divide into 2 equal portions. Form into 2 tight round loaves and place on the pan. Cover loosely with plastic wrap and let rise at room temperature until puffy but not quite double in bulk, about 30 minutes. These loaves will expand considerably in the oven.

5] Meanwhile, preheat the oven to 375°F.

6] Bake in the center of the oven until the loaves are golden brown and sound hollow when tapped, 35 to 40 minutes. Remove from the pan and place on a rack over a piece of wax paper to catch the drips while glazing.

7] To prepare the glaze: In a small bowl using a whisk, combine the powdered sugar, milk or spirit, and vanilla if using milk. Beat to form a glaze that is smooth and thick, but pourable. Adjust the consistency of the glaze by adding more liquid a few drops at a time. Pour the glaze over the surface of the still-hot loaf, letting the extra drip down the sides. Cool on a rack before slicing.

Decorating Pan de Muerto *in the Traditional Manner*
In Step 4, divide the dough into thirds, with 2 larger pieces equal in size to form the loaves and a small piece for the decorations. Refrigerate the small piece and form the remaining 2 pieces into round loaves as directed. Cover with plastic wrap and set aside. (This loaf may also be formed into a thick crucifix.) Press both loaves to form flatish rounds no more than 1 inch thick on the baking sheet. Remove the reserved dough from the refrigerator and place on the work surface. Divide the dough into 3 sections.

To make bones, roll 3 pieces of dough into fat cylinders, then roll with your hands to lengthen in the middle. Tears are formed from the remaining dough section by rolling small balls and pinching the ends. One larger ball, the skull, traditionally crowns the bread with the bones arranged in a cross joined to the skull. The tears are sprinkled in the empty spaces. Press firmly to make the decorations adhere and glaze with an egg beaten with 1 teaspoon milk or water. Let the loaves rise as in Step 4.

Halfway through baking, remove the bread from the oven and quickly brush once more with the egg glaze. Sprinkle lavishly with coarse sugar or colored crystal sugar squares. Return to the oven. Continue to bake and cool as in the recipe.

THREE KINGS BREAD RING

Rosca de los Reyes

In the Southwest, as in many parts of the world, January 6, Three Kings' Day, also called Twelfth Night or Epiphany, is celebrated with as much fanfare as Christmas. A freeform crown of orange-scented egg dough is baked and decorated with jewel-like preserved fruits. A tiny figurine representing the Christ child is baked into the bread as a good luck charm. Whoever gets the piece with the charm is named king or queen for the day and is obliged to host a party on El Día del la Candelaria, *February 2.*

MAKES I RING LOAF

Sponge
¾ cup warm milk (105° TO 115°F.)
½ cup warm water (105° TO 115°F.)
Pinch of sugar
1 tablespoon (1 package) active dry yeast
1 cup unbleached all-purpose flour

Dough
3 to 3¼ cups unbleached all-purpose flour
¼ cup sugar
Grated zest of 2 oranges
1½ teaspoons salt
3 eggs
1 teaspoon pure vanilla extract or 1 small
    vanilla bean, split lengthwise
3 tablespoons orange brandy, such as Grand Marnier
½ cup (1 stick) unsalted butter, at room temperature,
    cut into pieces
½ cup dried currants
½ cup chopped candied orange rind,
    preferably homemade
8 ounces mixed candied fruits or chopped
    Honey-glazed Dried Fruit *(See page 66)*
1 or large pecan half, whole almond, or whole dried fig

Sugar Crystal Glaze
1 egg yolk, lightly beaten
10 pecan halves or whole almonds
10 pieces crystallized angelica
3 tablespoons unsalted butter, melted
¼ cup granulated or large-crystal decorating sugar
    (See Note)

1] *To prepare the sponge:* In a large bowl with a whisk or in the bowl of a heavy-duty electric mixer fitted with the paddle attachment, combine the milk, water, and sugar. Sprinkle with the yeast and stir to dissolve. Let stand until foamy, about 5 minutes. Sprinkle with the flour and beat on low speed until smooth. Scrape down the sides and cover with plastic wrap. Let stand at room temperature until bubbly, about 2 hours.

2] *To prepare the dough:* In a large bowl with a whisk or in the bowl of a heavy-duty electric mixer fitted with the paddle attachment, combine 1½ cups of the flour, the sugar, orange zest, and salt. Add the sponge, eggs, vanilla (or scrape out the seeds from the split vanilla bean into the bowl), orange brandy, and butter pieces. Beat on medium speed until creamy, about 2 minutes. Add the remaining flour, ½ cup at a time, mixing on low speed until a soft dough that just clears the sides of the bowl forms, switching to a wooden spoon as necessary if making by hand.

3] Turn out the dough onto a lightly floured work surface and knead until the dough is soft and springy, 1 to 2 minutes for a machine-mixed dough and 3 to 5 minutes for a hand-mixed dough, adding 1 tablespoon flour at a time as necessary to prevent sticking. The dough should not be too dry. Place in a greased deep container, turn once to coat the top, and cover with plastic wrap. Let rise at room temperature until double in bulk, about 2 hours. Do not rush this dough, as the full rising time is important to develop the flavor and texture.

4] Grease or line a 15-inch pizza pan with parchment paper. Turn out the dough onto a clean work surface and pat into a fat rectangle. Sprinkle with the dried, candied and glazed fruits and press in with your palms. Roll into a cylinder and then smooth into a thick rope, 20 to 22 inches long. Insert the charm into the bottom of the dough and pinch to close. Lay on the pan and pinch the ends together with water-moistened fingers to form a closed ring. Grease the outer sides of a 6-inch cake pan and place it upside down in the center of the ring to keep the center hole from closing up. Loosely cover with plastic wrap and let rise at room temperature until double in bulk, about 1 hour.

5] About 20 minutes before baking, preheat the oven to 375°F.

6] *To glaze the ring:* Brush the entire surface with the egg yolk and gently press the nuts and angelica in a decorative pattern into the top. Bake in the center of the oven until browned and a cake tester inserted into the center comes out clean, 40 to 45 minutes. Remove from the oven and brush with the melted butter and sprinkle with the sugar. Turn off the oven and return the ring to the oven for 5 minutes. Remove immediately and let stand for 10 minutes. Use a large spatula to carefully transfer from the pan to a rack. Cool completely before slicing.

NOTE: Decorating sugar is available from cake-decorating stores.

HONEY-GLAZED DRIED FRUIT
Makes about 8 ounces glazed fruit

> 1¼ cups sugar
> ¼ cup honey
> 2 tablespoons light corn syrup
> ½ cup water
> 8 ounces dried fruit, such as apple slices, whole figs,
>   and/or apricot, pear, or peach halves

1] In a deep heavy saucepan, combine the sugar, honey, corn syrup, and water. Heat over low heat, stirring constantly with a wooden spoon, until the sugar dissolves, about 5 minutes. Using a pair of metal tongs, add the fruit, taking care not to splash. Bring the mixture to a boil without stirring. Immediately reduce the heat to medium and simmer the syrup. Cook the fruit slowly for 15 minutes exactly, stirring gently to avoid burning and basting occasionally. The fruit will plump up.

2] Remove the pan from the heat and immediately place in a pan of warm water to cool the syrup slightly. Carefully remove the individual pieces of fruit with tongs, letting the extra syrup drip off back into the pan. Place on wax paper or parchment paper set on a wire rack to cool completely, at least 8 hours. (Store in an airtight container separated by sheets of wax paper or parchment paper that has been brushed with a thin film of corn syrup for up to 3 weeks in the refrigerator.)

SOUTHWEST EGG BREAD

Pan de Huevos

This bread is good sliced thick and oven-dried until crisp and golden brown. Known as biscocho, *it was a standard food to carry on buffalo hunts and trips. The dough can also be formed into a dozen round rolls, arranged in two greased nine-inch pie plates.*

MAKES TWO 8½-BY-4½-INCH LOAVES

½ cup warm water (105° TO 115°F.)
1 tablespoon (1 package) active dry yeast
Pinch of granulated sugar
4 large eggs
3 tablespoons unsalted butter or lard, melted
½ cup (packed) dark brown sugar or 1 cone
    piloncillo, crumbled
2 teaspoons salt
4 to 4½ cups unbleached all-purpose flour
Rich Egg Glaze (page 127)

1] Pour the water into a small bowl or 1-cup liquid measuring cup. Sprinkle the yeast and sugar over the surface of the water. Stir to dissolve and let stand at room temperature until foamy, about 10 minutes.

2] In a large bowl using a whisk or in the bowl of a heavy-duty electric mixer fitted with the paddle attachment, combine the eggs, butter, brown sugar, salt, and 2 cups of the flour. Add the yeast mixture and beat on medium speed until smooth, about 1 minute. Add the remaining flour, ½ cup at a time, mixing on low speed until a soft shaggy dough that just clears the sides of the bowl forms, switching to a wooden spoon when necessary if making by hand.

3] Turn the dough out onto a lightly floured work surface and knead until a soft, smooth, and elastic dough forms, 1 to 2 minutes for a machine-mixed dough and 3 to 4 minutes for a hand-mixed dough, dusting with flour only 1 tablespoon at a time, just enough as needed to prevent sticking. The dough will be firm to the touch and slightly springy. Place in a greased deep container, turn once to coat the top, and cover with plastic wrap. Let rise at room temperature until double in bulk, 2 to 2½ hours.

4] Lightly grease the bottom and sides of two 8½-by-4½-inch loaf pans, (use clay pans if you have them). Turn the dough out onto the work surface and divide into 4 equal portions. With your palms, roll each section into a 12-inch log. Twist 2 sections of dough around each other to form a 2-strand braid. Repeat with the remaining portions to form a second loaf. Place in the loaf pans. Cover loosely with plastic wrap and let dough rise until fully double in bulk, 1 to 1½ hours.

5] About 20 minutes before baking, preheat the oven to 350°F.

6] Brush the surface of the loaves with the glaze. Bake for 35 to 40 minutes, or until the tops are golden brown, the sides slightly contract from the pan, and the loaf sounds hollow when tapped with your finger. Immediately remove from the pans to cool on racks.

HOMEMADE WHITE BREAD

Pan Casero

Early Spanish recipes called for home-boiled red cane sugar syrup, similar to light molasses or treacle, in place of the honey. You could bake the dough in a dozen individual size loaves in 4-by-2½-inch strap loaf pans. This bread is the base for the classic New Mexican Bread Pudding (See page 72).

MAKES 2 ROUND OR 8½-BY-4½-INCH LOAVES

⅓ cup warm water (105° TO 115°F.)
1 tablespoon (1 package) active dry yeast
Pinch of sugar
1 can (13 ounces) warm evaporated goat's milk
    (105° TO 115°F.)
2 tablespoons honey or light molasses
2 tablespoons lard or unsalted butter, melted
4 to 4½ cups unbleached all-purpose flour or
    bread flour
2 teaspoons salt
2 tablespoons melted lard or unsalted butter,
    for brushing

1] Pour the water into a small bowl or 1-cup liquid measuring cup. Sprinkle the yeast and sugar over the surface of the water. Stir to dissolve and let stand at room temperature until foamy, about 10 minutes.

2] In a large bowl using a whisk or in the bowl of a heavy-duty electric mixer fitted with the paddle attachment, combine the milk, honey, lard, and 1½ cups of the flour. Add the yeast mixture and beat on low speed for about 1 minute, or until smooth. Add the remaining flour, ½ cup at a time, mixing on low speed until a soft shaggy dough that just clears the sides of the bowl forms, switching to a wooden spoon when necessary if making by hand.

3] Turn the dough out onto a lightly floured work surface and knead until soft and springy, 1 to 2 minutes for a machine-mixed dough and 3 to 5 minutes for a hand-mixed dough, dusting with flour only 1 tablespoon at a time, just enough as needed to prevent sticking. The dough will be smooth and springy. Place in a greased deep container, turn once to coat the top, and cover with plastic wrap. Let rise at room temperature until double in bulk, about 1½ hours.

4] Lightly grease the bottom and sides of two 8½-by-4½-inch loaf pans (use clay pans if you have them), or grease or line a baking sheet with parchment paper. Turn the dough out onto the work surface and divide into 2 equal portions. Form into rectangular or round loaves, and place in the prepared pans. Cover loosely with plastic wrap and let the dough rise until it reaches the top of the pan, about 1 hour.

5] About 20 minutes before baking, preheat the oven to 350°F.

6] Brush the surface of the loaves with the melted lard or butter. Bake for 35 to 40 minutes, or until the tops are golden brown, the sides slightly contract from the pan, and the loaf sounds hollow when tapped with your finger. Immediately remove from the pans to cool on racks.

FRENCH-STYLE MEXICAN HARD ROLLS

Bolillos

In the 1860s during French rule in Mexico, the Emperor
Maximillian brought his own bakers over from Europe. One
of the living artifacts of that period is the bolillo *roll, similar in
shape to a weaving spindle. A bit sweeter and softer than its
French* petit pain *counterpart, this roll is now an integral part
of daily Southwest Mexican baking. Although the roll may be
made from any lean French- or Italian-style plain dough, the
following recipe uses a short sponge starter for a great-tasting roll.*

MAKES 20 ROLLS

Sponge
1½ tablespoons (1½ packages) active dry yeast
¼ cup sugar
3 cups warm water (105° TO 110°F.)
4 cups unbleached all-purpose flour

Dough
1 tablespoon salt
6 tablespoons (¾ stick) butter or vegetable shortening,
    at room temperature
3 to 3½ cups unbleached all-purpose flour
Egg Glaze (page 127)

1] *To prepare the sponge:* Sprinkle the yeast and sugar over
the water in a 3- or 4-quart bowl or plastic container and
stir until dissolved. Let stand until foamy, about 10 minutes.
Add the 4 cups of unbleached flour. With a whisk, beat
hard until smooth and thick. Scrape the sides with a spatula.
Cover loosely with plastic wrap and let stand at room
temperature, about 1 hour. The sponge will be bubbly.

2] *To prepare the dough:* Add the salt, butter, and ½ cup
of the flour to the sponge. Beat hard with a whisk for

5 minutes, or 2 minutes on medium speed in the bowl of
a heavy-duty electric mixer fitted with the paddle attachment. Add the remaining flour, ½ cup at a time, mixing on
low speed until a soft dough that just clears the sides of the
bowl forms, switching to a wooden spoon as necessary if
making by hand.

3] Turn dough out onto a lightly floured surface and
knead vigorously to create a soft, moist, and elastic dough
that will still feel sticky, 2 to 4 minutes, adding flour only
1 tablespoon at a time as needed. Use a dough scraper to
clean off the film of dough that accumulates on the work
surface as you go along. Take care not to add too much
flour; this dough should just hold its shape, yet retain a
slightly moist quality. Place the dough in a deep greased
container, turn once to coat the top, and cover with plastic
wrap. Let rise at room temperature until double in bulk,
1 to 1½ hours.

4] Grease or line 1 or 2 baking sheets with parchment
paper. Turn the dough out onto a lightly floured work
surface and divide into 2 equal portions. Divide each
portion into 10 equal portions. Pat each one into a 3-by-
2-inch rectangle and roll up to form into a tight oval. Pinch
the seams to seal and arrange about 2 inches apart on the
pans. Pinch the ends, pulling slightly, to form a spindle
shape. Cover loosely with plastic wrap and let rise at room
temperature until double in volume, about 30 minutes.

5] About 20 minutes before baking, preheat the oven to
400°F., with a baking stone or tiles on the lowest rack.

6] Using a sharp knife, gently slash the rolls with a lengthwise cut down the middle, no deeper than ¼ inch. Brush
the top of each roll with the glaze. Place the baking sheet
directly on the hot stone and bake for 10 minutes. Brush
the rolls again with the wash. Reduce the oven temperature
to 375°F. and bake for 15 to 18 minutes more, or until
the tops are golden brown and the rolls sound hollow

when tapped with your finger. Remove from the pans immediately to a cooling rack. They are best slightly warm or at room temperature, broken with the hands into pieces. *(Bolillos* may be frozen for up to 1 month.)

VARIATION
Mexican Flat Bread Rolls (Teleras): Prepare the dough through Step 4. Divide into 20 portions. Flatten the ball of dough into an oval with the heel of your hand or a rolling pin. Press twice into the top of the roll with the side of your hand to make 2 indentations. Let rise and press again to re-form the indentations. Bake and cool as directed.

Preheat the oven to 350°F. Toast the bread for 10 minutes. Beginning with a layer of toast, alternate layers of toast, cheese, raisins, and nuts in a 9-by-12-inch baking dish. Set aside. In a large saucepan, combine the brown sugar, water, vanilla, cinnamon, and cloves. Bring to a boil to dissolve the sugar. Reduce the heat and simmer, uncovered, for 15 minutes. Add the butter, stirring to melt. Pour the hot syrup over the bread layers in the baking dish, evenly soaking the entire contents and pressing to allow the bread to soak up the syrup. Cover tightly with foil and bake in the center of the oven for 50 minutes to 1 hour, or until firm. Serve warm, at room temperature, or cold.

NEW MEXICAN BREAD PUDDING
Capirotada

The brown sugar syrup used in this bread pudding is a classic ingredient in Mexican desserts. The pudding may be served with a pitcher of heavy cream, a brandied hard sauce, or plain yogurt.

SERVES 8

1 loaf day-old homemade white bread, cut into
    ½-inch slices and torn into large pieces
1 pound Longhorn cheddar cheese, thickly shredded or
    1 cup cheddar and 1 cup cream cheese
½ cup raisins, chopped dried figs, or dried wild Canyon
    grapes, soaked in hot water 15 minutes and drained
½ cup piñon (pine nuts) or chopped pecans
2 cups (packed) light brown sugar or 4 cones *piloncillo*
6 cups water
1 tablespoon pure vanilla extract
1 tablespoon ground cinnamon
Pinch of ground cloves
2 tablespoons unsalted butter

SWEET SAFFRON ROLLS
Molletes de Azafrán

These little buns have a long history in the Spanish Southwest. Daily bread would be enriched with animal fat, sugar or honey, and spices, including saffron or azafrán, (wild safflower), which is less potent in flavor than true saffron but still bright in color, then formed into simple round rolls. The dough may also be made into a braided loaf. If you want to dust with the flavored sugar, make it the day before and let it steep overnight in a closed container.

MAKES 24 ROLLS

½ cup unbleached all-purpose flour
½ cup blanched almonds
1½ tablespoons (1½ packages) active dry yeast
Pinch of sugar
11/4 cups warm water (105° TO 115°F.)
½ teaspoon crumbled saffron threads, ⅛ teaspoon
    powdered saffron, or 2 tablespoons *azafrán*
½ cup granulated sugar
4 large eggs
2 teaspoons salt

5 to 5½ cups unbleached all-purpose flour
¾ cup (1½ sticks) unsalted butter, at room
    temperature and cut into pieces
Rich Egg Glaze (page 127)
½ cup saffron-flavored sugar for dusting (optional)
    (See Note)

1] In a food processor, combine the ½ cup unbleached flour and almonds and process until a coarse flour is formed. Set aside. In a small bowl, sprinkle the yeast and the pinch of sugar over ½ cup of the warm water. Stir to dissolve. Let stand until foamy, about 10 minutes. In another bowl, combine the remaining water with the saffron. Let steep for 10 minutes.

2] In a large bowl with a whisk or in the bowl of a heavy-duty electric mixer fitted with the paddle attachment, combine the granulated sugar, almond flour, saffron water, eggs, salt, and 1 cup of the unbleached flour. Beat on medium speed until creamy, about 1 minute. Add the yeast mixture and ½ cup more flour. Beat on medium speed 1 minute more. Add the butter pieces and beat until incorporated. Add the remaining flour, ½ cup at a time, mixing on low speed until a soft dough that just clears the sides of the bowl forms, switching to a wooden spoon as necessary if making by hand.

3] Turn out the dough onto a lightly floured work surface and knead until smooth and elastic, 1 to 2 minutes for a machine-mixed dough and 3 to 5 minutes for a hand-mixed dough, adding only 1 tablespoon flour at a time as necessary to prevent sticking. Do not add too much flour or the rolls will be tough. Place dough in a deep greased container, turn once to coat the top, and cover with plastic wrap. Let rise at room temperature until double in bulk, 1 to 1½ hours. Grease or line 1 or 2 baking sheets with parchment paper.

4] Turn the dough out onto a lightly floured work surface. Divide the dough into 2 equal portions. Divide each portion into 12 equal portions. Form each into a tight round. Arrange, barely touching each other, on the prepared pans. Cover loosely with plastic wrap and let rise at room temperature until puffy, about 30 minutes.

5] About 20 minutes before baking, preheat the oven to 350°F.

6] Brush each bun with glaze. Bake in the center of the oven until the rolls are golden brown, 12 to 16 minutes. Remove to a rack to cool. Serve warm or at room temperature, dusted with sifted saffron-flavored sugar, if desired.

Note: To make saffron-flavored sugar, stir a pinch of crumbled saffron threads or powder or 1 teaspoon *azafrán* into ½ cup powdered sugar and let stand overnight.

VARIATION

Saffron Egg Braid: Prepare the dough through Step 3. Turn the dough out onto a lightly floured work surface and divide into 2 equal portions. Divide each portion into 3 equal portions. Form each into a 12-inch rope. Lay 3 ropes parallel to each other and braid without stretching the dough, going from the middle to each end. Pinch the ends together and tuck under. Place the braids at least 2 inches apart on the pans. Let rise at room temperature until puffy, about 30 minutes. Bake for 40 to 45 minutes, or until golden brown and a cake tester inserted into the center of the bread comes out clean. Remove to a rack to cool completely before serving. Dust with sifted saffron-flavored sugar, if desired. Makes 2 braids.

MEXICAN MORNING BUNS
Pan Dulce

Every Mexican panadería *north and south of the border has
its selection of this round sweet bun in a variety of shapes and
sizes with different toppings, from icings to brightly colored pink or
red sugar crystals. I think this homemade* Pan Dulce *is definitely
superior to the bakery version; it's more substantial and less sweet.
You can have the buns with a chocolate or cinnamon-vanilla
crunchy topping. If you are traveling close to the border, try to find
the authentic rustic-looking metal cutters for stamping out designs
into the topping. The most common designs are the* concha
(seashell swirl) and the crosshatch; shapes are the elote *(ear of
corn) and the* cuerno *(crescent).*

MAKES 16 BUNS

Dough
¼ cup warm water (105° TO 115°F.)
1 tablespoon (1 package) active dry yeast
Pinch of sugar
⅔ cup warm whole milk (105° TO 115°F.)
5 large eggs
2 teaspoons pure vanilla extract
⅔ cup sugar
1 teaspoon salt
4 to 4½ cups unbleached all-purpose flour
6 tablespoons (¾ stick) unsalted butter, at room
    temperature, cut into pieces

Sugar Topping
1 cup unbleached all-purpose flour
1 cup powdered sugar
½ cup (1 stick) unsalted butter or margarine, at room
    temperature and cut into pieces
1 large egg, beaten
1 large egg yolk, beaten
1 tablespoon pure vanilla extract

¼ cup unsweetened cocoa powder
1½ tablespoons ground cinnamon

1 egg white beaten with 1 teaspoon water for brushing

1] *To prepare the dough:* Pour the water into a small bowl
or 1-cup liquid measuring cup. Sprinkle the yeast and the
pinch of sugar over the surface of the water. Stir to dissolve
and let stand at room temperature until foamy, about 10
minutes.

2] In a large bowl using a whisk or in the bowl of a heavy-
duty electric mixer fitted with the paddle attachment,
combine the milk, eggs, vanilla, sugar, salt, and 2 cups of
the flour. Add the yeast mixture and beat on medium speed
until smooth, about 1 minute. Add the butter pieces and
mix on low speed to incorporate, 15 seconds. Add the
remaining flour, ½ cup at a time, mixing on low speed
until a soft shaggy dough that just clears the sides of the
bowl forms, switching to a wooden spoon when necessary
if making by hand.

3] Turn the dough out onto a lightly floured work surface
and knead until a soft, smooth, and elastic dough form, 1 to
2 minutes for a machine-mixed dough and 3 to 4 minutes
for a hand-mixed dough, dusting with flour only 1 tablespoon at a time, just enough as needed to prevent sticking.
The dough will be firm to the touch and springy. Place in a
greased deep container, turn once to coat the top, and cover
with plastic wrap. Let rise at room temperature until double
in bulk, 1 to 1½ hours.

4] *To prepare the sugar topping:* In a small bowl with your
fingers or with a heavy-duty electric mixer or in a food
processor, combine the flour and sugar. Sprinkle the vanilla,
egg and egg yolk over the dry mixture and add the butter
pieces. Mix or process quickly to make a soft, crumbly
mixture. Divide into 2 equal portions, adding the cocoa
to one and the cinnamon to the other. Set aside, covered.

5] Grease or line 1 or 2 large baking sheets with parchment paper. Turn the dough out onto a lightly floured work surface and divide into 16 equal portions.

6] Form each portion into a tight round and press to flatten the round to about 3 inches in diameter. Place all the rolls on the baking sheets. Divide the topping into 16 portions, half chocolate and half cinnamon. Greasing your hands, roll each portion into a ball. Pat or roll each out into a circle that will fit on top of a roll. Press on top of the ball of dough, making certain the circle sticks. Using the tip of a small sharp knife or a *Pan Dulce* cutter, cut a crisscross or curved shell pattern into the topping.

7] Cover loosely with plastic wrap and let rise at room temperature until puffy, 40 minutes.

8] About 20 minutes before baking, preheat the oven to 375°F.

9] Bake the rolls in the center of the oven for 15 to 18 minutes, or until golden brown and firm to the touch. Remove from the pan to cool on a rack. Serve immediately warm or at room temperature.

VARIATION

Elotes: Prepare the dough and topping through Step 5. Roll a portion of dough into an elongated oval. Sprinkle with 2 tablespoons of the sugar filling and roll up. Place, seam side down, on the baking sheet and pull up the open lips of dough at one end to form an ear. Slash each ear lengthwise with a paring or small sharp knife to open slightly. Place 2 inches apart on the baking sheet. Continue with Steps 7, 8, and 9.

Cuernos: Prepare the dough and topping through Step 5. Roll a portion of the dough into an 8-by-4-inch oval; sprinkle with 2 tablespoons of the filling. Roll up from the long side to make a thick log. Hold both ends and twist in opposite directions, making 6 twists, then curve into a crescent. Place 2 inches apart on the prepared pans. Continue with Steps 7, 8, and 9.

SWEET PUMPKIN ROLLS

Molletes de Calabaza

Fresh and dried strips of winter squash have been a favorite ingredient in Spanish baking since the settlers were introduced to the crop by the Natives. Pumpkin was usually mixed with nuts and raisins for pie and empanada fillings as well as for yeast and quick breads. The squash is both sweetened and spiced in these soft yeast rolls.

MAKES 26 ROLLS

7 to 7½ cups unbleached all-purpose flour
1 cup (packed) light brown sugar or 2 cones
    piloncillo, crumbled
4 teaspoons active dry yeast
2 teaspoons salt
1 teaspoon ground cinnamon
1 teaspoon freshly grated nutmeg
1 teaspoon ground allspice
¼ teaspoon ground cloves
1 cup hot water (120°F.)
¼ cup vegetable oil
1½ cups pumpkin or other winter squash puree,
    canned or homemade (page 141)
1 cup currants

Spiced Brown Sugar Topping
1 cup (packed) light brown sugar or 2 cones
    piloncillo, crumbled
1 teaspoon ground cinnamon
½ teaspoon ground cloves
½ teaspoon freshly grated nutmeg
Egg Glaze (page 127)

1] In a large mixing bowl with a whisk or in the bowl of a heavy-duty electric mixer fitted with the paddle attachment, combine 2 cups of the unbleached flour, sugar, yeast, salt, and spices. Add the hot water and beat on medium speed for 1 minute, or until creamy. Beat in the oil, pumpkin, and currants. Add the remaining unbleached flour, ½ cup at a time, until a soft dough that just clears the sides of the bowl forms, switching to a wooden spoon as necessary if making by hand.

2] Turn the dough out onto a lightly floured work surface and knead until smooth, springy, and soft, 1 to 3 minutes, adding only 1 tablespoon flour at a time as necessary to prevent sticking. Transfer the dough to a greased deep container, turn once to coat the top, and cover with plastic wrap. Let rise at room temperature until double in bulk, 1½ to 2 hours.

3] Grease or line a 16-by-10-inch roasting pan or baking sheet with parchment paper. Turn the dough out onto a lightly floured work surface and divide into 2 equal portions. Divide each into 13 equal portions. Form each portion into a tight ball. Place with the sides just touching in the pan. Cover loosely with plastic wrap and let rise at room temperature until double in bulk, about 40 minutes. The rolls will be puffy and look like small cushions.

4] To prepare the sugar topping: In a small bowl, combine the sugar and spices until evenly blended. Set aside.

5] About 20 minutes before baking, preheat the oven to 375°F.

6] Brush the rolls with the glaze. Using your thumb, gently make an indentation in the top of each roll. Spoon in a heaping teaspoon of the spiced brown sugar. Bake the rolls in the center of the oven for 25 to 30 minutes, or until golden brown and firm to the touch. Remove from the pan to cool on a rack.

SAVORY EMPANADAS

Empanadas are baked or fried turnovers made from a short pastry or yeasted bread dough. They are a fundamental part of Southwest baking and are eaten at all holiday feasts and festivals. This recipe is for a three-bite-size savory empanada. Empanadas can be deep-fried, but I prefer to bake them. This is a yeasted pastry, but you can also use the pastry in the Mincemeat Empanandas, substituting savory spices for the sweet ones. You have a choice here of two different fillings.

MAKES 14 TO 16 TURNOVERS

2 teaspoons active dry yeast
Pinch of sugar
1 cup warm water (105° TO 115°F.)
2 teaspoons New Mexico chile powder
1 teaspoon ground cumin
½ teaspoon salt
3 tablespoons olive oil
2 to 2¼ cups unbleached all-purpose flour
¼ cup yellow cornmeal, for rolling out dough
Potato and Cheese Filling (recipe follows)
Sausage Filling (recipe follows)
Vegetable oil, for brushing

1] In a medium bowl, sprinkle the yeast and sugar over ½ cup of the warm water. Stir to dissolve and let stand until bubbly, about 10 minutes. Add the remaining water, chile powder, cumin, salt, oil, and 1 cup of the flour. Beat with a whisk until smooth. Add the remaining flour, ½ cup at a time, until a soft shaggy dough that just clears the sides of the bowl forms, switching to a wooden spoon when necessary if making by hand. The dough should be moist, yet hold together when kneaded a few times into a round. Place in a greased container, cover with plastic wrap, and let rise at room temperature until puffy, about 1 hour. (The dough can be refrigerated, wrapped in plastic wrap, for up to 1 day.)

2] Grease or line two 16-by-10-inch baking sheets with parchment paper. On a work surface lightly dusted with the cornmeal, roll the pastry out to a 20-by-16-inch rectangle, ⅛ to ¼ inch thick. Using a 4-inch biscuit cutter or clean tuna fish can with both ends cut out, cut out rounds. Reroll excess dough and cut out more rounds. Place 1 heaping tablespoon of filling onto the center of each round. Moisten the edge of the dough with water and fold over to make a half-moon. Crimp the edges with the tines of a fork or scallop with your fingers by flipping sections of the edge in toward the center and twisting to seal (a technique known as *repulgar* in Tex-Mex baking). Place the pastries 1 inch apart on the pans. Brush the tops with oil. Let stand, uncovered, for 20 minutes at room temperature, or until puffy.

3] Meanwhile, preheat the oven to 400°F.

4] Using a fork, pierce the tops of the empanadas a few times to allow the steam to escape. Bake in the center of the oven for 12 to 16 minutes, or until golden brown and dry to the touch. Remove from the pan with a metal spatula and place on a rack to cool.

POTATO AND CHEESE FILLING
Makes enough for 1 batch of empanadas

1 large onion, chopped
1 tablespoon olive oil
About 1¼ pounds new potatoes, boiled, peeled,
    and cut into small cubes (2 cups)
1 tablespoon New Mexico red chile powder
Salt, to taste
8 ounces soft fresh goat cheese

In a large skillet over medium heat, sauté the onion in
the olive oil until translucent, about 5 minutes. Add the
potatoes, chile powder, and salt. Cool to room temperature
before using. Sprinkle the filling with cheese when filling.
(Filling may be made ahead and refrigerated overnight.)

SAUSAGE FILLING
Makes enough for 1 batch of empanadas

1 pound spicy sausage meat, such as New Mexican
    sausage or chorizo
2 medium mild green chiles, such as Anaheim,
    seeded, deveined, and chopped
3 scallions, chopped
1 can (6 ounces) pitted black olives, chopped
2 plum tomatoes, seeded and chopped
Black pepper, to taste
2 cups shredded Longhorn cheddar cheese (optional)

In a large skillet over medium heat, sauté the sausage meat
and chiles until the meat is no longer pink and the chile is
soft. Drain and discard the fat. Transfer to a medium bowl
and add the scallions, olives, tomatoes, pepper, and cheese,
if using. Refrigerate as long as overnight. Use chilled.

NEW

SOUTHWEST

BAKERY

I go on
calling
nana to
the Earth

feeding on
the subversive
canto sown
by los antiguos

inside
the humblest
tortillas
of life

FRANCISCO X. ALARCÓN, *"Canto a las Tortillas,"*
from *Snake Poems* (Chronicle Books, 1992)

An ocean lover or city dweller may find it difficult to imagine the alchemy of brilliant sunshine, sharp dry heat, mesa dust, and archaeological ruins in the Southwest. Yet it draws tourists from around the world. The avant garde of the 1920s fell in love with New Mexico, and the area became a mecca for artists—musicians, writers, poets, and painters—whose faithful chronicles brought the Southwest to the attention of the rest of the country.

The modern hospitality industry strives to accommodate tourists while bakeries try to keep up with the local demand for Native American Indian and Spanish breads.

Luckily, the Southwest is home to stubborn bakers, and traditional Native and Hispanic family breads are now very much back in fashion. Many restaurants and small eateries serve bread made from their own recipes and baked on the premises. Innovative breads are served side by side with traditional breads.

Hotels in Taos and Santa Fe are known for their blue cornmeal breakfast pancakes and breads. Tecolote, the Santa Fe breakfast hot spot, serves exotic sounding atole-piñon pancakes—simply blue cornmeal and pine nuts. The Coyote Café in Santa Fe uses stone-ground flours for its buckwheat and whole wheat breads. The Boulders resort in Phoenix offers guests yellow corn bread packed with cheeses and green chiles as snacks. The Inn of the Anasazi's Navajo flatbread topped with fire-roasted sweet peppers is a favorite of the locals as well as tourists. Tucson's Café Terra Cotta makes focaccia and blue corn–laced breads. And all of these restaurants serve stacks of tortillas with meals. The Three Angels Bakery outside of Las Cruces makes eight types of breads without any added fat or sugar, including a raised green chile cornmeal loaf, and offers mail-order shipping.

Southwest-inspired food seems to travel well, too. Mark Miller's Red Sage in Washington, D.C., serves breadsticks infused with chili powder, and New York's Arizona 206 has cushiony blue corn muffins on its daily menu. Saint Estèphe in Manhattan Beach, California, serves blue corn sticks artistically peeking out of fresh corn husks. Zuni Cafe, a popular eatery in San Francisco, has adobelike walls, wood-fired ovens, and bright Navajo-style decor.

The Santa Fe School of Cooking offers tours and classes, including seminars in adobe oven baking demonstrated at the historic Rancho de las Golindrinas in La Cienega. La Casa Córdova, the oldest adobe home in Tucson, is a Hispanic Heritage Museum which retains its original *cocina,* equipped with raised adobe platforms and immense metal *comals* suspended over open fires for tortilla baking.

The restaurant at the Hopi Cultural Center on Second Mesa, staffed by Hopi women, serves fry bread, *mumuozpiki* dumplings, steamed grits called *huzrusuki,* and stacks of hearty gray-blue cornmeal and *saquavikavike* pancakes year round. Piki bread, which must be savored in its home environs to be totally appreciated, is handmade there by local bakers. The Pueblo Cultural Center in Albuquerque has its own restaurant, the Pueblo Kitchen Restaurant, staffed with Native cooks who serve up authentic breads and foods. During the winter they offer a traditional Pueblo feast, complete with fry and pueblo yeast bread, blue corn breads, tamales, and savory cornmeal gruels.

Tortillerias, such as the Estrella Tortilla Factory in Phoenix, and "mexicatessens" in every major Southwest city offer handmade corn and flour tortillas available fresh throughout the day. Restaurants and food emporiums have wheat and corn tortillas brought in from the numerous quality *tortillerias.* Rancho de Chímayo in New Mexico fries hundreds of puffy sopaipillas daily. Restaurants may take shortcuts by making sopaipillas out of Bisquick (Huntley Dent recommends ¼ cup water to 1½ cups mix in case you want to try this) or a high-quality mix sold by a mill such as Valencia Mills (available from the Old Southwest Trading Company).

In traditional Mexican bakeries, self service is the rule. The La Jolla Bakery in Tucson is known as one of the best. Armed with metal tongs and tray, you pick your own sweet or savory buns.

Travelers hit the high road between Taos and Santa Fe to Ranch O Casados for their smoky blue corn tortilla flour. I often find Los Chileros blue corn flour in ethnic markets; it seems to glisten with a rainbow of luminescent colored specks.

The Desert Botanical Garden in Phoenix and the Tucson Botanical Garden are dedicated to locating and preserving ancient strains of food plants. They further educate the public on the cornucopia of local wild foods by offering classes in desert baking, using amaranth, mesquite, and acorn meal in muffins, breads, and pancakes. A glimpse into the future and past at the same time, WildWheat is cultivated from an indigenous saltgrass cereal crop *(trigo geutil),* long grown by Natives at the mouth of the Colorado River before the building of the dam, that can tolerate water with high salinity and tolerate extreme temperatures.

Although some Native American communities still do not have electricity, the introduction of electric grain grinders, food processors, refrigerators, freezers, and electric stoves has had its affect on ancestral ways. But the communal pueblos all retain their old ways of storage and piki preparation and the old corn-grinding rooms. For native festivals and religious celebrations the venerable milling rooms are still used for grinding corn by hand and the old outdoor ovens are fired up with juniper and piñon wood for bread baking.

Today's Southwest style of baking takes lots of poetic license with local ingredients, but the techniques remain essentially pure. It is simple and rustic, yet sophisticated at the same time. It is a style that is building in momentum and popularity.

PIONEER SOURDOUGH BREAD

Before commercial yeast, bakers used starters to make bread rise. In Southwest ranch, lumber camp, and mining town kitchens, bubbling crocks of naturally fermenting sourdough starters were used to make pancakes, biscuits, and breads for every meal. Since chuck wagon bakers on the trail often had no equipment, breads were mixed by making a well into the top of a sack of flour and adding the starter and salt to make a dough.

MAKES TWO 9-BY-5-INCH LOAVES

1½ cups warm water (105° TO 115°F.)
1 tablespoon (1 package) active dry yeast
1 tablespoon sugar
1 cup sourdough starter or yogurt starter
½ cup (1 stick) unsalted butter, margarine,
    or lard, melted
1 tablespoon salt
5½ to 6 cups unbleached all-purpose flour or
    bread flour
¼ cup fine yellow or white cornmeal, for sprinkling

1] Pour ½ cup of the warm water into a small bowl or 1-cup liquid measuring cup. Sprinkle the yeast and a pinch of the sugar over the surface of the water. Stir to dissolve and let stand at room temperature until foamy, about 10 minutes.

2] In a large bowl using a whisk or in the bowl of a heavy-duty electric mixer fitted with the paddle attachment, combine the sourdough starter, the remaining water, remaining sugar, melted butter, salt, and 3 cups of the flour. Beat on medium speed until smooth, about 1 minute. Add the yeast mixture and beat on medium speed for 1 minute more. Add the remaining flour, ½ cup at a time, until a soft shaggy dough that just clears the sides of the bowl forms, switching to a wooden spoon when necessary if making by hand.

3] Turn the dough out onto a lightly floured work surface and knead until smooth and elastic, 1 to 2 minutes for a machine-mixed dough and 3 to 4 minutes for a hand-mixed dough, dusting with flour only 1 tablespoon at a time, just enough as needed to prevent sticking. Place in a greased deep container, turn once to coat the top, and cover with plastic wrap. Let rise at room temperature until double in bulk, 1 to 1½ hours.

4] Lightly grease the bottom and sides of two 9-by-5-inch loaf pans (use clay loaf pans if you have them), and sprinkle with the cornmeal. Turn the dough out onto the work surface and divide it into 2 equal portions. Form into rectangular loaves and place in the prepared pans. Cover loosely with plastic wrap and let rise until double in bulk, with the dough about 1 inch above the rim of the pans, about 1 hour.

5] About 20 minutes before baking, preheat the oven to 350°F.

6] Bake in the center of the oven for 35 to 40 minutes, or until the tops are golden brown, the sides slightly contract from the pan, and the loaves sound hollow when tapped with your finger. Immediately turn out of the pans onto a rack and cool completely before slicing.

VARIATIONS

Add 1 to 2 cups raisins or dried blueberries, 1 cup of granola, or 1 cup of chopped pitted black olives to the dough in Step 2.

SOURDOUGH STARTERS

In the old Southwest, bakers used various starters—rye sourdough starts with a raw onion submerged; salt starters, for which the starter mixture stood on heated rock salt to keep the temperature stable; raw or mashed potato starters; starters activated with dry hops; starters from crushed fresh grapes; and the yeast-rich frothy foam that was skimmed off the top of beer and ale and then propagated in potato water. Dough from the last batch of bread containing these starters would be saved to leaven each new batch of dough.

To make a starter, also called a mother or chef, mix flour and water or milk and leave the mixture to stand at room temperature. The invisible wild yeast spores in the air will propagate in this medium and begin to ferment or sour. The mixture will bubble and expand with enzyme action and smell slightly sour and apple-like from the malolactic fermentation (the same process as in wine production). Some geographic locations are better for getting a strong starter, as pollution seems to decrease the potency of the wild yeast. If your batter does not bubble within a few days, add a pinch of cultivated yeast.

When the starter is ready, it is mixed with more liquid and flour to make a sponge. The sponge is then left to ferment before being mixed into a bread dough. The starter-sponge method provides leavening and acidic flavor. It takes about six months for a sourdough starter to develop a good, strong flavor.

A starter must be replenished after each use or if it has been inactive. To keep a sourdough starter in good condition, use it about every 2 weeks. It should never be completely used up in building a dough, and it should be replenished every time it is used. Never add salt, as it retards the natural enzyme activity.

Replenishing the starter: Let the starter come to room temperature. Stir the separated liquid back into the mixture and discard half if only feeding, or use the amount called for in the recipe to prepare the sponge. Pour the rest into a small bowl. Add equal amounts (usually ½ , ¾, or 1 cup) of unbleached or whole wheat flour and liquid (milk, water, potato water, or plain yogurt), and a large pinch of sugar, honey, or maple syrup for food. Mix into a thick, creamy mass. Wash out the starter glass container or pottery crock with hot water. Return the starter to the container and cover with several thicknesses of cheesecloth held in place with a rubber band. Alternatevely, pinch off a small section (about ½ cup) of the kneaded dough. Drop it into the starter jar and let stand, uncovered, for 2 days before covering and refrigerating.

Let stand until bubbly, stirring several times a day, overnight or for up to 2 days at room temperature, depending on how sour you want the starter to be. It will bubble and expand, rise and fall, smell slightly sour and apple-like. Do not leave the starter at room temperature longer than 5 days without replenishing. If the starter turns pink, the milk has broken down and needs to be discarded. Scoop off the colored portion and replenish. After fermenting, return the starter to the refrigerator, covered with a layer of plastic wrap held in place with a rubber band.

PAN PUEBLO

This is my version of an outdoor horno-style bread especially suited for baking in a home oven. It can also be baked in a terra cotta cloche baker (La Cloche), if you have one. You can score the loaf before it goes into the oven, but traditional loaves are baked smooth.

MAKES 1 LARGE OVAL LOAF

1½ cups warm milk (105° TO 115°F.)

2½ teaspoons (1 scant package) active dry yeast

½ cup sugar

¼ cup olive oil or sunflower seed oil

2 teaspoons salt

4 to 4½ cups unbleached all-purpose flour or bread flour

3 tablespoons yellow cornmeal, for sprinkling

1] Pour in ¾ cup of the warm milk into a small bowl or 1-cup liquid measuring cup. Sprinkle the yeast and a pinch of the sugar over the surface of the water. Stir to dissolve and let stand at room temperature until foamy, about 10 minutes.

2] In a large bowl using a whisk or in the bowl of a heavy-duty electric mixer fitted with the paddle attachment, combine the remaining ¾ cup milk, remaining sugar, oil, salt, and 1 cup of flour. Beat on medium speed until smooth, about 1 minute. Add the yeast mixture and beat on medium speed for 1 minute more. Add the remaining flour, ½ cup at a time, until a soft shaggy dough that just clears the sides of the bowl forms, switching to a wooden spoon when necessary if making by hand.

3] Turn the dough out onto a lightly floured work surface and knead until firm yet still springy, 1 to 2 minutes for a machine-mixed dough and 3 to 5 minutes for a hand-mixed dough, dusting with flour only 1 tablespoon at a time, just enough as needed to prevent sticking. Place in a greased deep container, turn once to grease the top, and cover with plastic wrap. Let rise at room temperature until double in bulk, 1 to 1½ hours. Lightly grease or line a baking sheet with parchment paper and sprinkle with the cornmeal. Or use a 12-inch perforated pizza pan tin.

4] Turn the dough out onto the work surface and form into a tight oval. Place the loaf on the baking sheet and cover loosely with plastic wrap. Let rise until double in bulk, about 45 minutes.

5] About 20 minutes before baking, preheat the oven to 400°F. For best results, line the bottom and top racks of the oven with a large baking stone or tiles to create a mini stone oven.

6] Bake on the stone, or if not using a stone, bake in the center of the oven for 10 minutes. Reduce the heat to 350°F. and bake for 20 to 25 minutes more, or until golden brown and the loaf sounds hollow when tapped with your finger. Transfer the loaf to a rack to cool before slicing.

VARIATION

Green Chile Baguettes: Prepare the dough through Step 3. Turn the dough out onto the work surface and divide into 3 equal portions. Roll or pat each section into a large rectangle no thicker than 1 inch. Spread each with one third of the Green Chile Paste (recipe follows), leaving a 1-inch margin all around the dough. Roll up, jelly-roll fashion, from the long side. Pinch the seams and sides. Place, seam down, on the baking sheet. Cover loosely with plastic wrap and let rest for 20 minutes. Preheat the oven to 400°F., with a baking stone, if desired. Using a sharp knife, slash the tops with 3 diagonals, no deeper than ¼ inch. Bake in the center of the oven for 30 to 35 minutes, or until deep brown and crusty. Serve warm. Makes 3 loaves.

GREEN CHILE PASTE

Green chile paste is a staple in Southwest kitchens, a coarse puree mashed by hand in a mortar and pestle and used extensively in sauces and stews, and even as a sandwich spread.

MAKES ABOUT 1½ CUPS

¼ cup corn oil
1 small white onion, chopped
1 clove garlic, chopped
4 poblano or New Mexico green chiles, roasted,
    peeled, and seeded (page 137)
⅓ cup (lightly packed) fresh cilantro leaves
½ cup pine nuts
Juice of 1 lime
¼ cup grated parmesan
Yellow cornmeal, for dusting

In a small skillet, heat the corn oil. Sauté the onion and garlic until soft. Remove from the heat and cool. Transfer to a food processor, scraping in all of the oil. Add the remaining ingredients and pulse until a coarse paste is formed. Set aside. (The paste will keep for 1 week in the refrigerator topped with a thin layer of oil or frozen in small airtight containers for 2 months.)

POTATO BREAD WITH SOUTHWEST HERBS

The fluffy, moist character of potato bread is a soft blanket wrapped around a thin line of bright green spirited flavor. Use plenty of parsley, going lighter on the more assertive aromatic leaves such as the epazote, Mexican mint marigold, oregano, and bergamot, herbs that have been grown for centuries in the traditional Southwest kitchen garden, the huerta familiar.

MAKES TWO 9-BY-5-INCH LOAVES

1 large (8 ounces) baking potato
1 tablespoon (1 package) active dry yeast
3 tablespoons honey
6½ to 7 cups unbleached all-purpose flour
    or bread flour
1 cup warm milk (105° TO 115°F.)
2 large eggs
⅓ cup olive oil
1 tablespoon salt
4 tablespoons (½ stick) unsalted butter or lard,
    at room temperature
1½ cups (lightly packed) chopped mixed fresh herbs
    such as parsley, Mexican oregano, cilantro, mint,
    marjoram, sage, bergamot, Mexican mint marigold,
    or epazote
Rich Egg Glaze (page 127)

1] Peel the potato and cut into large pieces. Place in a 2-quart saucepan and cover with water. Bring to a boil and cook until soft. Drain, reserving ½ cup of the potato water. Rice or mash the potato and set aside to cool. (You should have 1 cup.) Warm or cool the potato water to 105° to 115°F. and pour into a small bowl. Sprinkle the yeast and a teaspoon of the honey over the potato water. Stir to combine and let stand until foamy, about 10 minutes.

2] In a large bowl using a whisk or in the bowl of a heavy-duty electric mixer fitted with the paddle attachment, combine 2 cups of the flour, the remaining honey, milk, eggs, oil, salt, mashed potatoes, and yeast-potato water. Beat on medium speed hard until creamy, about 1 minute. Add the remaining flour, ½ cup at a time, and mix on low speed until a soft shaggy dough that just clears the sides of the bowl forms, switching to a wooden spoon when necessary if making by hand.

3] Turn the dough out onto a lightly floured work surface and knead until soft and springy, 1 to 2 minutes for a machine-mixed dough and 3 to 5 minutes for a hand-mixed dough, dusting with flour only 1 tablespoon at a time, just enough as needed to prevent sticking. The dough will be smooth and springy. Do not let it get too dry by adding too much flour or the loaf will be very heavy. Place the dough in a greased deep container, turn the dough once to coat the top, and cover with plastic wrap. Let rise at room temperature until double in bulk, 1½ to 2 hours.

4] Lightly grease the bottom and sides of two 9-by-5-inch loaf pans. Place the herbs in a small bowl and toss to combine evenly. Turn the dough out onto a lightly floured work surface and without working it further, divide it into 2 equal portions. Roll or pat each portion of dough into a rough rectangle and spread each with half of the soft butter. Sprinkle each with half of the chopped herbs and roll up into a loaf shape. Place the loaves, seam side down, in the loaf pans. Cover loosely with plastic wrap and let rise at room temperature until the dough is fully double in bulk and about 1 inch over the rims of the pans, about 45 minutes.

5] About 20 minutes before baking, preheat the oven to 375°F.

6] Brush the surfaces with glaze. Using a sharp knife, make 3 diagonal slashes across the top of each loaf, no more than

¼ inch deep. Place the pans in the center of the oven and bake for 40 to 45 minutes, or until the tops are golden brown, the sides slightly contract from the pan, and the loaves sound hollow when tapped with your finger. Remove the loaves from the pans immediately to a cooling rack. Loaves are best slightly warm or at room temperature.

CORNMEAL PUEBLO BREAD WITH WALNUTS

This loaf bears no resemblance to baking powder corn bread, which is quite crumbly. Rather, it is a crusty country bread with walnuts added to complement the corn. Use Arizona walnuts, which are similar to black walnuts, or black walnuts, if you can get them. The recipe calls for a fine grind of cornmeal, such as that used for making tortillas. If possible, use one of the special blue cornmeals ground from Hopi, Jemez, Isleta, Casados Blue, Blue Squaw, or Taramuhara Maíz Azul flour corn. Seeds for these are available to the home gardener from Native Seed/SEARCH. (See page 148).

MAKES 1 LARGE OR 2 MEDIUM ROUND LOAVES

2½ cups warm water (105° to 115°F.)
1½ tablespoons (1½ packages) active dry yeast
Pinch of sugar
⅓ cup corn oil or melted unsalted butter
1 tablespoon salt
¾ cup whole wheat flour
1¼ cups fine-grind yellow or blue cornmeal
1¼ cups walnuts, preferably Arizona or black walnuts, lightly toasted and chopped
3¾ to 4¼ cups unbleached all-purpose flour or bread flour
3 tablespoons *each* whole wheat flour and yellow or blue cornmeal, combined, for sprinkling

1] Pour ½ cup of the warm water into a small bowl or 1 cup liquid measuring cup. Sprinkle the yeast and sugar over the surface of the water. Stir to dissolve and let stand at room temperature until foamy, about 10 minutes.

2] In a large bowl using a whisk or in the bowl of a heavy-duty electric mixer fitted with the paddle attachment, combine the remaining 2 cups water, oil, salt, whole wheat flour, and cornmeal. Beat on medium speed until smooth, about 1 minute. Add the yeast mixture and beat on medium speed vigorously 1 minute longer. Add the toasted walnuts and 1 cup of the unbleached flour. Continue to add the flour, ½ cup at a time, mixing on low speed until a soft shaggy dough that just clears the sides of the bowl forms, switching to a wooden spoon when necessary if making by hand.

3] Turn the dough out onto a lightly floured work surface and knead in flour until a soft grainy-textured dough forms, 1 to 2 minutes for a machine-mixed dough and 3 to 5 minutes for a hand-mixed dough, dusting with flour only 1 tablespoon at a time, just enough as needed to prevent sticking. The dough will hold its own shape, yet retain a soft springy quality. Place in a greased deep container, turn once to coat the top, and cover with plastic wrap. Let rise at cool room temperature until double in bulk, 1½ to 2 hours.

4] Line a baking sheet or wooden peel with parchment paper and sprinkle with the combined whole wheat flour and cornmeal. Turn the dough out onto a lightly floured work surface and shape into 1 or 2 tight round loaves. Place on the baking sheet or wooden peel, seam side down. Cover loosely with plastic and let rise until double in bulk, about 1 hour.

5] About 20 minutes before baking, preheat the oven to 400°F., placing a baking stone on the bottom rack, if desired.

6] Rub the top of the loaf gently to coat lightly with flour, and using a sharp knife, slash the top of the loaves 4 times to form a square pattern, no deeper than ¼ inch. Slide the loaf onto the hot stone or place the baking sheet directly on the stone. If not using a stone, bake in the middle of the oven. Reduce the heat to 375°F. Bake 45 to 50 minutes, or until the loaf is crusty brown and sounds hollow when tapped with your finger. Cool completely on a rack.

BUTTERMILK CORNMEAL BREAD WITH FRESH CHILES AND CHEDDAR

This is my version of a bold loaf served at the Coyote Café in Santa Fe, New Mexico. The flavors of the fresh chiles are worth the little bit of work it takes to prepare them, so don't skip this bread because of that step.

MAKES TWO 8½-BY-4½-INCH LOAVES

¾ cup warm water (105° TO 115°F.)
1 tablespoon (1 package) active dry yeast
Pinch of sugar
2 serrano chiles, seeded, deveined, and minced
1 poblano chile, seeded, deveined, and minced
½ red bell pepper, seeded, deveined, and minced
1 cup grated Longhorn cheddar cheese
1½ cups warm buttermilk (105° TO 115°F.)
¼ cup corn oil
2 tablespoons honey
1 tablespoon salt
1½ teaspoons ancho chile powder
⅓ cup coarse-grind yellow cornmeal, polenta,
   or *masa harina para tamales*
¾ cup fine-grind white cornmeal or
   masa harina para tortillas
¾ cup whole wheat flour

4 to 4½ cups unbleached all-purpose flour
   or bread flour

1] Pour the warm water into a small bowl or 1-cup liquid measuring cup. Sprinkle the yeast and sugar over the surface of the water. Stir to dissolve and let stand at room temperature until foamy, about 10 minutes. Meanwhile, combine the serrano chiles, poblano chile, bell pepper, and cheese in a small bowl and set aside.

2] In a large bowl using a whisk or in the bowl of a heavy-duty electric mixer fitted with the paddle attachment, combine the buttermilk, oil, honey, salt, chile powder, yellow and white cornmeal, and whole wheat flour. Beat on medium speed until smooth, about 1 minute. Add the yeast mixture and beat on medium speed 1 minute more. Stir in the chile-cheese mixture. Add the remaining all purpose flour, ½ cup at a time, mixing on low speed until a soft dough that just clears the sides of the bowl forms, switching to a wooden spoon when necessary if making by hand. Do not work the dough so vigorously that the chiles lose their shape.

3] Turn the dough out onto a lightly floured work surface and knead until smooth and elastic, 1 to 2 minutes for a machine-mixed dough and 3 to 5 minutes for a hand-mixed dough, dusting with flour only 1 tablespoon at a time, just enough as needed to prevent sticking, and pushing back in any bits of chile or cheese that fall out. The dough will retain a nubby, slightly tacky quality. Place in a greased deep container, turn once to coat the top, and cover with plastic wrap. Let rise at room temperature until double in bulk, 1½ to 2 hours.

4] Lightly grease the bottom and sides of two 8-by-4-inch loaf pans. Turn the dough out onto the work surface and divide into 2 equal portions. Form into rectangular loaves and place in the pans. Cover loosely with plastic wrap and let rise until doubled in bulk and the dough is about 1 inch above the rim of the pans, about 45 minutes.

5] About 20 minutes before baking, preheat the oven to 375°F.

6] Bake in the center of the oven for 45 to 50 minutes, or until the tops are golden brown, the sides slightly contract from the pan, and the loaves sound hollow when tapped with your finger. Immediately turn out of the pans onto a rack and cool completely before slicing.

NIXTAMAL BREAD

Created by my friend food writer Janet Fletcher, this is the only recipe I have ever come across for using hominy, also called nixtamal in a yeast bread. This dough can be patted out, brushed with olive oil, and layered with strips of roasted green chiles before rolling up jelly-roll fashion for a savory swirled loaf. It is a wonderfully moist, flavorful loaf.

MAKES TWO 8½-BY-4½-INCH LOAVES

½ cup warm water (105° TO 115°F.)
1 tablespoon (1 package) active dry yeast
¼ cup sugar
2 cups cooked hominy (see page 21),
   or 1 can (16-ounces) hominy, rinsed
1 cup milk
2 tablespoons unsalted butter or lard, melted
2 teaspoons salt
4½ to 5 cups unbleached all-purpose flour or
   bread flour
White or yellow cornmeal, for dusting

1] Pour the ½ cup of warm water into a small bowl or 1-cup liquid measuring cup. Sprinkle the yeast and a pinch of the sugar over the surface of the water. Stir to dissolve and let stand at room temperature until foamy, about 10 minutes.

2] Combine the hominy and milk in a saucepan and heat to 100°F. Transfer to a food processor and puree until slightly chunky.

3] In a large bowl using a whisk or in the bowl of a heavy-duty electric mixer fitted with the paddle attachment, combine the hominy-milk mixture, the remaining sugar, melted butter, salt, and 1 cup of the flour. Beat on medium speed until smooth, about 1 minute. Add the yeast mixture and beat on medium speed 1 minute more. Add the remaining flour, ½ cup at a time, mixing on low speed until a soft shaggy dough that just clears the sides of the bowl forms, switching to a wooden spoon when necessary if making by hand.

4] Turn the dough out onto a lightly floured work surface and knead until smooth and elastic, 1 to 2 minutes for a machine-mixed dough and 3 to 4 minutes for a hand-mixed dough, dusting with flour only 1 tablespoon at a time, just enough as needed to prevent sticking. Place in a greased deep container, turn once to coat the top, and cover with plastic wrap. Let rise at room temperature until double in bulk, 1 to 1½ hours.

5] Lightly grease the bottom and sides of two 8½-by-4½-inch loaf pans (use clay pans if you have them), and sprinkle all sides lightly with cornmeal. Turn the dough out onto the work surface and divide into 2 equal portions. Form into rectangular loaves and place in the pans. Cover loosely with plastic wrap and let rise until doubled in bulk, with the dough about 1 inch above the rim of the pans, about 1 hour.

6] About 20 minutes before baking, preheat the oven to 375°F.

7] Bake in the center of the oven for 35 to 40 minutes, or until the tops are golden brown, the sides slightly contract from the pan, and the loaves sound hollow when tapped with your finger. Immediately turn out of the pans onto a rack and cool completely before slicing.

YEASTED SOPAIPILLAS

These light little hollow "pillows" of dough are similar to Navajo fry bread. Most recipes call for baking powder and frying; this yeast-risen version was originally served at Fred Harvey's La Fonda in Santa Fe. I have adapted it to be baked in the oven, rather than deep-fried. La Fonda offered sopaipillas as an afternoon repast with hot Mexican chocolate or coffee and chango, *cream cheese with guava jelly and steamed and sugared guava peels.*

MAKES 24 LITTLE SOPAIPILLAS

¼ cup warm water (105° TO 115°F.)
1 tablespoon (1 package) active dry yeast
Pinch of sugar
About 3 cups unbleached all-purpose flour
1 teaspoon salt
2 tablespoons sugar
¾ cup milk
1 large egg
2 tablespoons solid vegetable shortening or
    unsalted butter, melted

1] Pour the warm water into a small bowl or 1-cup liquid measuring cup. Sprinkle the yeast and the pinch of sugar over the surface of the water. Stir to dissolve and let stand at room temperature until foamy, about 10 minutes.

2] In a large bowl with a whisk or in the bowl of a heavy-duty electric mixer fitted with the paddle attachment, combine 2¾ cups of the flour, the salt, and 2 tablespoons sugar. Add the yeast, milk, egg, and melted shortening or butter. Beat on medium speed until smooth, about 1 minute.

3] Turn the dough out onto a lightly floured work surface and knead gently just until smooth, about 10 kneads, adding flour 1 tablespoon at a time as necessary to prevent sticking. Dough must remain very soft. Place in a greased deep container, turn once to grease the top, and cover with plastic wrap. Let rise at room temperature for about 45 minutes or in the refrigerator for about 2 hours. The dough may be refrigerated at this point for up to 48 hours, but it should be deflated daily.

4] Preheat the oven to 500°F. Line 2 baking sheets with parchment paper.

5] Place the dough on a lightly floured work surface and divide it into quarters. Gently roll each section of dough out ⅛ to ¼ inch thick. Fold the dough in half and gently reroll it. Do this 2 times. Let the dough rest for a few minutes if it becomes too springy or hard to handle. With a dough wheel or very sharp knife, cut each section of dough into 6 squares, oblongs, triangles, or diamonds. The shapes can be irregular, but they should be about 2 by 3 inches. Place on a lightly floured baking sheet and cover loosely with plastic wrap. If you work quickly, the dough can stay at room temperature for up to 5 minutes; otherwise refrigerate it until ready to bake or up to overnight.

6] Place the dough pieces on the baking sheets, at least 1 inch apart. Bake in the center of the oven, 1 pan at a time, until puffed and brown, 8 to 10 minutes. Serve warm.

VARIATION

Substitute ½ cup fine-grind white, yellow, or blue cornmeal or mesquite flour (see page 140) for ½ cup of the all-purpose flour.

RED AND GREEN CHILE BRIOCHE

Red pepper flakes and roasted green chiles are added to an egg- and butter-rich yeast dough to make a fine-textured dinner or sandwich roll. The dough is chilled overnight, so plan on making the dough the day before you intend to bake them. Look for strap pans (a set of twelve attached mini loaf pans) or baby brioche tins to make these individual loaves especially charming.

MAKES 12 MINI LOAVES

4½ cups unbleached all-purpose flour
1 tablespoon (1 package) active dry yeast
2 tablespoons sugar
1 tablespoon crushed red pepper
2 teaspoons salt
½ cup hot water (120°F.)
1 to 2 fresh mild green chiles, such as New Mexico
    or poblano, roasted, peeled, seeded, and diced
    (see page 137), to make ⅔ cup
5 large eggs, at room temperature
¾ cup (1½ sticks) unsalted butter, at room temperature,
    cut into small pieces

1] In the bowl of a heavy-duty electric mixer fitted with the paddle attachment, combine 1 cup of the flour, the yeast, sugar, red pepper, and salt. Add hot water and beat at medium speed for 2 minutes, or until smooth. Add the green chiles and beat on medium speed until evenly distributed. Add the eggs, one at a time, beating well after each addition. Gradually add 2 cups more of the flour on low speed. When well blended, add the butter a few pieces at a time. Beat just until incorporated. Gradually add exactly 1½ cups of the remaining flour, beating on low speed for about 2 minutes. Beat until thoroughly blended and creamy. The dough will be very soft and have a batterlike consistency.

2] Scrape the dough into a large greased bowl or deep plastic container. Cover tightly with plastic wrap and let rise at a cool room temperature until doubled in bulk, about 3 hours. Gently deflate the dough, cover tightly, and refrigerate for 12 hours or overnight.

3] Lightly grease 12 mini loaf pans. Turn the chilled dough out onto a lightly floured surface and divide it into 16 equal portions. Form into small oblong loaves and place in the prepared pans. Cover with plastic wrap and let rise at cool room temperature until double in bulk, 1 to 1½ hours.

4] About 20 minutes before baking, preheat the oven to 375°F.

5] Bake in the center of the oven until golden brown, 20 to 25 minutes. Remove from the pans to cool completely on a rack before serving.

CORNMEAL CRESCENT DINNER ROLLS

These yeasted cornbread crescents are moist and light-textured with a little crunch. Day-old rolls are good for bread puddings or toasted with melted cheese.

MAKES 24 CRESCENTS

¼ cup water (105° to 115°F.)
1 tablespoon (1 package) active dry yeast
Few drops of honey or a pinch of sugar
1 cup warm milk (105° to 115°F.)
¼ cup corn oil
1 tablespoon honey or sugar
2 teaspoons salt
1 large egg
1 cup yellow or blue cornmeal, fine- or medium-grind
1½ teaspoons dried oregano or sage leaves, crumbled (optional)
3 to 3½ cups unbleached all-purpose flour or bread flour

1] Pour the warm water into a small bowl or 1-cup liquid measuring cup. Sprinkle the yeast and the drops of honey or pinch of sugar over the surface of the water. Stir to dissolve and let stand at room temperature until foamy, about 10 minutes.

2] In a large bowl with a whisk or in the bowl of a heavy-duty electric mixer fitted with the paddle attachment, combine the milk, oil, 1 tablespoon honey or sugar, salt, egg, and cornmeal. Beat on medium speed to make a smooth batter, about 2 minutes. Add the yeast mixture and dried oregano, if using. Add the flour, ½ cup at a time, mixing on low speed until a soft dough that just clears the sides of the bowl forms, switching to a wooden spoon if mixing by hand.

3] Turn the dough out onto a lightly floured work surface and knead until soft and springy, 1 to 2 minutes for a machine-mixed dough and 3 to 5 minutes for a hand-mixed dough, dusting with flour only 1 tablespoon at a time, just enough as needed to prevent sticking. Dough will feel a bit greasy and slightly sticky. Place in a deep greased container, turn once to grease the top, and cover with plastic wrap. Let rise in a warm place until double in bulk, about 2 hours.

4] Lightly grease or line 2 baking sheets with parchment paper. Gently deflate the dough, turn out onto a lightly floured surface, and divide into 3 equal portions. Roll or pat each into a circle about ¼ inch thick and cut each circle into 8 wedges. Roll wedges into a crescent shape from the long side to the point. Place, with the point down, 1 inch apart, on the prepared baking sheets. Cover loosely with plastic wrap and let rise until just double in bulk, about 30 minutes.

5] About 20 minutes before baking, preheat the oven to 375°F.

6] Bake for 12 to 16 minutes, or until golden brown. Cool on racks for at least 15 minutes before serving.

ANISE EGG BREAD

Southwest families have at least one anise-flavored yeast bread at Christmas season meals and parties. It is called pan de la riena, *or the queen's bread, in Spanish. It is light in texture from the eggs with a gently sweet flavor. This is celebratory food for feast days, a holdover for when the daily bread dough was enriched with lard, spices, sugar, and eggs.*

MAKES 3 BRAIDS OR 9-BY-5-INCH LOAVES

    1 tablespoon (1 package) active dry yeast
    1 cup sugar or honey
    2½ teaspoons salt
    6½ to 7 cups unbleached all-purpose flour or
        bread flour
    1½ cups hot water (120°F.)
    4 large eggs, slightly beaten
    10 tablespoons (1¼ sticks) unsalted butter or lard,
        melted
    1 tablespoon plus 1 teaspoon pure anise extract
    Grated zest of 1 large lemon
    Rich Egg Glaze (page 127)
    Whole anise seeds, for sprinkling

1] In a large bowl with a whisk or in bowl of a heavy-duty electric mixer fitted with the paddle attachment, combine the yeast, sugar, salt, and 2 cups of the flour. Add the water, eggs, butter, anise extract, and lemon zest. Beat hard with a whisk or on medium speed until smooth, 1 to 2 minutes. Scrape sides of bowl occasionally. Add the remaining flour ½ cup at a time, mixing on low speed to form a soft dough that just clears the sides of the bowl, switching to a wooden spoon when necessary if making by hand.

2] Turn the dough out onto a lightly floured work surface and knead until soft and springy, 1 to 3 minutes for a machine-mixed dough and 4 to 7 minutes for a hand-mixed dough, dusting with flour only 1 tablespoon at a time, just enough as needed to prevent sticking. The dough will be smooth and very springy. Take care not to add too much flour or the baked loaf will be dry and crumbly. A layer of blisters will show under skin and not feel sticky. The dough needs to be a bit firmer for freeform rather than pan loaves. Place in a greased deep container, turn once to coat the top, and cover tightly with plastic wrap. Let rise at room temperature until double in bulk, 1 to 1½ hours. (The dough may be gently deflated, covered tightly with 2 layers of plastic wrap, and refrigerated overnight, if desired. Remove from the refrigerator, gently deflate, and let rest at room temperature for about 1½ hours, before continuing.)

3] Lightly grease the bottom and sides of three 9-by-5-inch loaf pans. Turn the dough out onto a lightly floured surface and divide into 9 equal portions. Roll each portion into a 12-inch-long rope. Using 3 ropes for each braid, braid the ropes together from the middle. Taper the ends, tuck them under, and place each loaf into a loaf pan. Or place the loaves on a greased or parchment paper–lined baking sheet. Cover loosely with plastic wrap and let rise at room temperature until nearly doubled in bulk or 1 inch above the rim of the pans, 45 minutes to 1 hour. Because of the eggs, this loaf does not need to completely double, as it rises a lot in the heat of the oven.

4] About 20 minutes before baking, preheat the oven to 350°F.

5] Brush the tops with the glaze, taking care not to let it drip onto the pan. Sprinkle with the anise seeds. Bake in the center of the oven until deep golden brown, 50 to 55 minutes. Remove from the oven and immediately turn out onto a rack to cool completely before slicing. This bread freezes well.

VARIATION

Molletes de Anís: Prepare the dough through Step 2. Lightly grease or line 2 baking sheets with parchment paper. Turn the risen dough out onto the work surface and divide into 24 equal portions. Form each into a round ball. Place about 2 inches apart on the prepared pans. Let rise, uncovered, until fully double in bulk, about 1 hour. Bake in the center of the preheated 350°F. oven for 15 to 18 minutes, or until golden brown and hollow-sounding when tapped on the bottoms. Remove the pans to a rack set over a sheet of wax paper. Pierce each roll gently a few times with a bamboo skewer. Prepare 2 recipes of Brown Sugar Glaze (page 128). Pour 1 tablespoon of glaze over each roll. Let cool before serving. Makes 24 rolls.

FEAST DAY ANISE EGG BREAD

Feast days are large annual celebrations at the Indian pueblos and Spanish villages, honoring their patron saints. Homemade breads are very much part of the festivities. This loaf can also be baked in two angel food cake pans and coated with Honey Glaze (page 128).

MAKES 2 LARGE BRAIDS

2 cups mixed diced sundried, candied, or Honey-
   Glazed Dried Fruits (page 66) such as figs,
   pineapple, apricots, papaya, and apples
1 recipe Anise Egg Bread (page 98), prepared
   through Step 2
Rich Egg Glaze (page 127)

1] In a small bowl, combine the diced fruits and cover with boiling water. Let stand for 30 minutes to plump. Drain and pat dry with paper towels.

2] Lightly grease or line a baking sheet with parchment paper. Turn the dough out onto a lightly floured work surface and divide into 6 equal portions. Roll each portion into a 16-inch-long rope and flatten to 4 inches wide. Sprinkle each portion with ⅓ cup of the fruit. Roll up each portion jelly-roll fashion, from the long edge. Pinch the seam to seal. Be sure the ropes are of equal size and shape. Place 3 ropes parallel to each other. Braid the loaf, starting in the center and moving toward each end. Adjust or press the braid to fix any irregularities. Tuck the ends under and place the loaves on the pan, pinching the ends into tapered points. Cover loosely with plastic wrap and let rise at room temperature until the dough is almost double in bulk, about 40 minutes. This bread needs only a three-quarter proof before baking; if it rises more, it may collapse when baked. (The loaves may also be covered loosely with plastic wrap and left to rise in the refrigerator overnight. If you do this, let stand at room temperature for 1 hour before baking.)

3] About 20 minutes before baking, preheat the oven to 350°F. Bake and cool as directed in Step 5 on page 98.

4] Brush the surface with egg glaze.

PANOCHA-CINNAMON BREAD

The inspiration for this sweet bread comes from Classic
Southwest Cooking, *a wonderful cookbook by Carolyn Dille
and Susan Belsinger (Prima, 1994). Panocha flour, or sprouted
wheat flour, commonly seen during the Christmas holidays, is
used, although regular whole wheat flour can be substituted for it.
This is a compact, especially aromatic loaf.*

MAKES THREE 8½-BY-4½-INCH LOAVES

½ cup warm water (105° TO 115°F.)
1½ tablespoons (1½ packages) active dry yeast
Pinch of light brown sugar
4 to 4½ cups unbleached all-purpose flour or
    bread flour
1¼ cups panocha flour
½ cup (packed) light brown sugar
2½ teaspoons salt
1½ cups warm milk (105° TO 115°F.)
½ cup (1 stick) unsalted butter, melted
2 large eggs

Cinnamon Sugar
1⅓ cups (packed) light brown sugar
3 tablespoons ground cinnamon

6 tablespoons (¾ stick) unsalted butter, melted

1] Pour the warm water in a small bowl or 1-cup liquid
measuring cup. Sprinkle the yeast and the pinch of sugar
over the surface of the water. Stir to dissolve and let stand
at room temperature until foamy, about 10 minutes.

2] In a large bowl using the whisk or in the bowl of a
heavy-duty electric mixer fitted with a paddle attachment,
combine 1 cup of the all-purpose flour, the panocha flour,
brown sugar, and salt. Add the milk, melted butter, and eggs.

Beat at medium speed until creamy, about 1 minute. Stir
in the yeast mixture. Add the remaining unbleached flour
½ cup at a time, mixing on low speed until a sticky dough
that just clears the sides of the bowl forms, switching to a
wooden spoon when necessary if making by hand. The top
of the dough will be very moist. Be careful not to add too
much flour.

3] Turn the dough out onto a lightly floured work surface
and knead until very soft and springy, 30 seconds for a
machine-mixed dough and 1 to 2 minutes for a hand-
mixed dough, dusting with flour only 1 tablespoon at a
time, just enough as needed to prevent sticking. I usually
use less than 2 tablespoons. The dough will be a smooth
ball with a coarse surface, very springy and very moist.
Place the dough into a lightly greased deep container, turn
once to coat the top, and cover with plastic wrap. Let rise
at room temperature until double in bulk, 2 to 2½ hours;
this dough is a slow riser.

4] *To make the cinnamon sugar:* Combine the sugar and
cinnamon in a small bowl. Set aside.

5] Turn the dough out onto a lightly floured work surface
to deflate. Lightly grease the bottom and sides of three 8½-
by-4½-inch loaf pans. Without working the dough further,
use a sharp edge to divide it into 3 equal portions. Pat each
into a rough 12-by-10-inch rectangle of even thickness.
Brush each piece with 1½ tablespoons of the melted butter.
Sprinkle each with a third of the cinnamon sugar, leaving
a 1-inch border all the way around the edges. Beginning
at the short edge, roll up jelly-roll fashion into a tight log.
Pinch the ends and the long seam to seal to prevent the
sugar from leaking out while baking. Place the loaves,
seam side down, in the loaf pans. Brush the tops with the
remaining melted butter to prevent drying. Cover loosely
with plastic wrap and let rise at room temperature until
the dough is fully double in bulk and even with the rims
of the pans, about 1 hour.

6] About 20 minutes before baking, preheat the oven to 350°F.

7] Bake in the center of the oven for 40 to 45 minutes, or until the tops are evenly browned, the sides shrink from the pan, and the loaves sound hollow when tapped with your finger. Check the bottoms: they should be the same color as the top. Remove the loaves from the pans immediately to a cooling rack. Do not cut while hot. This bread is best slightly warm or at room temperature.

PUMPKIN-CINNAMON ROLLS

Squashes grow well in the warm Southwest climate and cook up into a brightly colored, silky textured bread. You can use any kind of pumpkin or other winter squash that is golden-orange in color in this sweet bread. Each one will have a different moisture and fiber content, so you will need to adjust the amount of flour you use. These rolls are spiral-shaped, echoing the petroglyphs in the archeological ruins of Chaco Canyon.

MAKES 12 ROLLS

Pumpkin Dough
1 tablespoon (1 package) active dry yeast
Pinch of light brown sugar
¼ cup warm water (105° TO 115°F.)
1 cup buttermilk
1 cup pumpkin or other winter squash puree, canned or homemade (page 141)
¼ cup (packed) light brown sugar
¼ cup corn oil
1 large egg
1 tablespoon salt
5 to 6 cups unbleached all-purpose flour or bread flour

Spiced Cinnamon Filling
¾ cup (packed) light brown sugar
¾ cup granulated sugar
3 tablespoons ground cinnamon
1½ teaspoons *each* ground ginger, nutmeg, and allspice
½ cup (1 stick) unsalted butter, melted, for brushing

Vanilla or White Chocolate Powdered Sugar Glaze (page 127)

1] *To make the dough:* In a small bowl or 1-cup liquid measuring cup, sprinkle the yeast and pinch of sugar over the surface of the water. Stir to dissolve and let stand at room temperature until foamy, about 10 minutes.

2] In a large bowl using a whisk or in the bowl of a heavy-duty electric mixer fitted with the paddle attachment, combine the buttermilk, pumpkin puree, brown sugar, oil, egg, salt, and 2 cups of the flour. Beat on medium speed until creamy, about 1 minute. Stir in the yeast mixture. Add the remaining flour ½ cup at a time mixing on low speed until a soft shaggy dough that just clears the sides of the bowl is formed, switching to a wooden spoon when necessary if making by hand.

3] Turn the dough out onto a lightly floured work surface and knead until soft and springy, 1 to 2 minutes for a machine-mixed dough and 3 to 5 minutes for a hand-mixed dough, dusting with flour only 1 tablespoon at a time, just enough as needed to prevent sticking. Leave the dough moist and semifirm, yet at the same time smooth and springy. Place in a greased deep container, turn once to coat the top, and cover with plastic wrap. Let rise at room temperature until double in bulk, 1½ to 2 hours.

4] *To prepare the filling:* In a small bowl, combine the sugars and spices. Set aside.

5] Grease or line 1 or 2 baking sheets with parchment paper. Turn the dough out onto a lightly floured work surface and divide it into 2 equal portions. Roll or pat each portion into a rectangle about 12-by-9 inches and ¾ inch thick. Leaving a 1-inch border all around the edges of the rectangle, brush the surface heavily with melted butter, then sprinkle evenly with the spiced sugar filling. Roll up jelly-roll fashion, starting from the long edge, and pinch the seam to seal. With a serrated knife using a gentle sawing motion, or a metal dough scraper using an even down motion, cut each roll into 9 equal portions, each portion being about 1½ inches thick. Place the slices on the baking sheet, cut side down, 1 inch apart. Cover loosely with plastic wrap and let rise at room temperature until puffy, about 45 minutes. Refrigerate, covered loosely with plastic wrap, for 2 to 24 hours. Let stand at room temperature for 15 to 20 minutes before baking.

6] About 20 minutes before baking, preheat the oven to 350°F.

7] Bake in the center of the oven until the tops are brown, 20 to 25 minutes. Remove from the oven and let rolls stand for 5 minutes on a wire rack.

8] Prepare the glaze, using as much sugar as needed to make a thick, smooth, spreadable frosting. Using a metal spatula, frost each roll. Let cool for at least 20 minutes before serving warm. (Rolls can be cooled completely, placed in individual sized plastic freezer bags, and frozen for 4 to 6 weeks.)

ORANGE-COCONUT SWEET ROLLS

Coconut and orange make an authentic Spanish-style stuffing for empanadas and sweet breads. Certainly these rolls need no butter or adornment other than the orange glaze that is drizzled over them.

MAKES 16 ROLLS

Sweet Dough
¼ cup warm water (105° TO 115°F.)
1 tablespoon (1 package) active dry yeast
Pinch of sugar
3 to 3½ cups unbleached all-purpose flour
¼ cup sugar
¾ teaspoon salt
6 tablespoons (¾ stick) unsalted butter,
    at room temperature
2 large eggs
½ cup sour cream
1 teaspoon pure vanilla extract

Orange Coconut Filling
1⅓ cups shredded sweetened coconut, toasted
    (See Note)
⅔ cup sugar
Grated zest of 2 large oranges
4 tablespoons (½ stick) unsalted butter, melted,
    for brushing
Orange Glaze
¼ cup sugar
¼ cup sour cream
2 tablespoons unsalted butter
2 tablespoons fresh orange juice

1] *To make the dough:* Pour the warm water into a small bowl or 1-cup liquid measuring cup. Sprinkle the yeast and the pinch of sugar over the surface of the water. Stir to dissolve and let stand at room temperature until foamy, about 10 minutes.

2] In a large bowl using a whisk or in the bowl of the heavy-duty electric mixer fitted with a paddle attachment, combine 1 cup of the flour, the sugar, and salt. Add the butter, eggs, sour cream, and vanilla. Beat on medium speed until creamy, about 1 minute. Stir in the yeast mixture. Add the remaining flour ½ cup at a time, mixing on low speed until a soft, shaggy dough that just clears the sides of the bowl forms. Switch to a wooden spoon when necessary if making by hand.

3] Turn the dough out onto a lightly floured work surface and knead until soft and springy, 1 to 2 minutes for a machine-mixed dough and 3 to 5 minutes for a hand-mixed dough, dusting with flour only 1 tablespoon at a time, just enough as needed to prevent sticking. The dough will be smooth and springy but not dry. Place in a greased deep container, turn once to coat the top, and cover with plastic wrap. Let rise at room temperature until double in bulk, 1½ to 2 hours.

4] *To prepare the filling:* Combine the coconut, sugar, and orange zest in a small bowl and toss to mix evenly. Set aside.

5] Grease or line a baking sheet with parchment paper. Turn out the dough onto the work surface and divide into 2 equal portions. Roll each half into a 12-inch circle. Brush each with 2 tablespoons of the melted butter and sprinkle with half of the filling. Divide each circle into 8 wedges with a sharp knife or pastry wheel. Roll each wedge up from the wide end toward the point. Place on the pans, point down, 2 inches apart. Cover loosely with plastic wrap and let rise at room temperature for 30 minutes.

6] About 20 minutes before baking, preheat the oven to 350°F.

7] Bake in the center of the oven for 15 to 20 minutes, or until puffy and golden brown. Remove from the oven and place the pan on a cooling rack.

8] *To prepare the glaze:* Combine the sugar, sour cream, butter, and orange juice in a small saucepan. Bring to a boil for exactly 3 minutes. The glaze will be thick and viscous. Immediately drizzle the warm rolls with the hot glaze and let stand until cool before serving.

NOTE: To toast coconut, scatter it over a parchment paper–lined baking sheet and toast in a 375°F. oven, stirring twice for even browning, until just golden brown, 6 to 8 minutes. Cool on the pan.

PANCAKES AND WAFFLES

Once known as "lightnin' breads," quick breads are economical as well as easy to mix and bake.
Pancakes and waffles were a staple of the old Southwest kitchen and are just as popular today. Old pioneer cookbooks
often contain a recipe for beer "sourdough" pancakes, an easy adaptation of early beer-based starters.

SOURDOUGH PANCAKES AND WAFFLES

Sourdough creates the Southwest's most delicate pancakes and waffles. A sponge is made the night before and the pancakes quickly mixed right before baking. If you are making these out camping, substitute water for the milk.

MAKES 20 PANCAKES OR 8 TO 10 WAFFLES

1 cup sourdough starter or yogurt starter
1½ cups milk
2 cups unbleached all-purpose flour
2 large eggs
2 tablespoons vegetable oil
1 teaspoon salt
1 teaspoon baking soda

1] *The night before:* In a medium nonreactive mixing bowl, combine the starter, milk, and 1 cup of the flour. Stir, but do not beat too much. Cover and refrigerate.

2] *In the morning:* Add the remaining flour, eggs, oil, salt, and baking soda to the sourdough mixture with a whisk, using a few swift strokes. Do not overmix. The batter should be the consistency of heavy cream and bubble due to the addition of the soda.

3] *For pancakes:* Heat a griddle or heavy skillet over medium heat until drops of water sprinkled on the surface dance over it. Lightly grease the griddle. Using a ¼-cup measure for each pancake, pour the batter onto the griddle. Cook until bubbles form on surface, the edges are dry, and the bottoms are golden brown, about 2 minutes. Turn once. The second side will take only 1 minute to cook. Serve at once or keep warm in a 200°F. oven until ready to serve.

4] *For waffles:* Preheat a waffle iron to medium-high heat or follow manufacturer's instructions. Grease the hot waffle iron grids (vegetable oil spray is excellent for this job) and without stirring down the batter, fill the iron halfway, about 1 cup for each waffle. Close the lid and bake until the waffle is golden brown and crisp, 3 to 4 minutes. Remove from the iron with a fork. Repeat with remaining batter. Keep waffles hot in a 200°F. oven, uncovered, until ready to serve. (Cooled waffles may be stored in plastic freezer bags and frozen for up to 2 months. Reheat in the toaster.)

VARIATION
Substitute 1 cup whole wheat flour for 1 cup of the all-purpose flour.

HARVEY GIRL ORANGE PANCAKES

꩜꩜꩜꩜꩜꩜

This is my adaptation of pancakes served in the Harvey Houses, dining facilities that were established on the Santa Fe railroad line from Kansas to California. The waitresses were called Harvey girls. These unique pancakes were originally made the size of a silver dollar.

MAKES ABOUT 16 PANCAKES

2 cups unbleached all-purpose flour
¼ cup sugar
1 tablespoon baking powder
½ teaspoon salt
2 large eggs
Grated zest of 2 oranges
1 cup fresh orange juice
1 cup milk
¼ cup vegetable oil
½ cup chopped fresh orange or tangerine sections

1] In a large bowl, combine the flour, sugar, baking powder, and salt. In another bowl, whisk together the eggs, zest, orange juice, milk, and oil. Combine the mixtures with a few swift strokes. Fold in the orange sections. Do not overmix. The batter will be thin.

2] Heat a griddle or heavy skillet over medium heat until drops of water sprinkled on the surface dance over it, then lightly grease. Using a ¼-cup measure for each pancake, pour the batter onto the griddle. Cook until bubbles form on the surface, the edges are dry, and the bottoms are golden brown, about 2 minutes. Turn once. The second side will take about 1 minute to cook. Serve at once or keep warm in a 200°F. oven until ready to serve.

BEER WAFFLES

꩜꩜꩜꩜꩜꩜

Use a Mexican beer, such as Dos Equis, to make these waffles. They will have the flavor of a mock sourdough and the beer will also serve as a leavening.

MAKES 6 TO 8 WAFFLES

2 cups unbleached all-purpose flour
1 cup whole wheat pastry flour
¼ cup (packed) light brown sugar
Grated zest of 1 lemon
1 teaspoon baking powder
½ teaspoon salt
2¾ cups beer, not flat
2 large eggs
½ cup (1 stick) unsalted butter, melted
1 tablespoon fresh lemon juice
4 teaspoons pure vanilla extract

1] In a large bowl, combine the unbleached flour, the whole wheat pastry flour, brown sugar, lemon zest, baking powder, and salt. In another bowl, combine the beer and eggs with a whisk. Pour into the dry mixture, stirring to moisten evenly. Gently stir in the melted butter, lemon juice, and vanilla. Refrigerate for 2 hours to overnight.

2] Preheat a waffle iron to medium-high heat or follow manufacturer's instructions. Grease the hot waffle iron grids (vegetable oil spray is excellent for this job) and without stirring down the batter, fill the iron halfway, about 1 cup for each waffle. Close the lid and bake until the waffle is golden brown and crisp, 4 to 5 minutes. Remove from the iron with a fork. Repeat with remaining batter. Keep waffles hot in a 200°F. oven, uncovered, until ready to serve. (Cooled waffles may be stored in plastic freezer bags and frozen for up to 2 months. Reheat in the toaster.)

BLUE CORNMEAL PANCAKES

Blue cornmeal pancakes show up on breakfast menus from El Tovar on the rim of the Grand Canyon to Santa Fe. They look very different from regular pancakes, a dusky shade of lavender-gray. One bite delivers the smoky sweetness of the ground roasted blue corn. Note that the recipe calls for the finest grind of blue-corn flour, often called harina para atole. *This recipe can also be used to make waffles.*

MAKES ABOUT 14 PANCAKES

1½ cups fine-grind blue cornmeal or *harina para atole*
¾ cup unbleached all-purpose flour or
    whole wheat pastry flour
1½ teaspoons baking powder
½ teaspoon baking soda
¼ teaspoon salt
2 large eggs
1½ cups buttermilk
¼ cup corn oil

1] In a large bowl, combine the blue cornmeal, unbleached flour, baking powder, baking soda, and salt. In another bowl, whisk together the eggs, buttermilk, and oil. Combine the mixtures with a few swift strokes. The batter should be the consistency of heavy cream. If too thick, add a few more tablespoons of buttermilk to thin.

2] Heat a griddle or heavy skillet over medium heat until drops of water sprinkled on the surface dances over it, then lightly grease. Using a scant ¼-cup measure for each pancake, pour the batter onto the griddle. Cook until bubbles form on surface, the edges are dry, and the bottoms are golden brown, about 2 minutes. Turn once. The second side will take only about 1 minute to cook. Serve at once or keep warm in a 200°F. oven until ready to serve.

VARIATIONS

Blueberry Blue Cornmeal Pancakes: Sprinkle about 2 tablespoons fresh or unthawed frozen blueberries over the surface of each pancake immediately after pouring onto the griddle. You will need about 1½ cups.

Blue Cornmeal Rice Pancakes: Add 1 cup cooked brown rice when mixing the batter in Step 1.

Savory Corn and Blue Cornmeal Pancakes: Thaw and drain 1 package (10 ounces) frozen baby corn kernels. Spoon 2 to 3 tablespoons of batter onto the griddle and sprinkle immediately with 1 tablespoon of the corn. Serve as a side dish for grilled meats and poultry.

ROASTED BANANA PANCAKES

Buy underripe bananas with green tips for baking in this recipe; save the all-yellow or flecked ones for eating out of hand or mashing into banana bread.

MAKES ABOUT 16 PANCAKES

2 medium underripe bananas, unpeeled
2 cups unbleached all-purpose flour
2 tablespoons sugar
2 teaspoons baking powder
1 teaspoon baking soda
¼ teaspoon salt
1¾ cups buttermilk
2 tablespoons vegetable oil
1 teaspoon pure vanilla extract
2 large eggs

1] Preheat the oven to 350°F.

2] Place the bananas on a baking sheet and roast for 20 minutes. Cool slightly, peel, and coarsely chop.

3] In a large bowl, combine the flour, sugar, baking powder, baking soda, and salt. In another bowl, whisk together the buttermilk, oil, vanilla, and eggs. Combine the mixtures with a few swift strokes. Do not overmix. Fold in the chopped bananas. The batter should be the consistency of heavy cream. If too thick, add a few more tablespoons of buttermilk to thin.

4] Heat a griddle or heavy skillet over medium heat until drops of water sprinkled on the surface dance over it, then lightly grease. Using a ¼ cup measure for each pancake, pour the batter onto the griddle. Cook until bubbles form on surface, the edges are dry, and the bottoms are golden brown, about 2 minutes. Turn once. The second side will take only 1 minute to cook. Serve at once or keep warm in a 200°F. oven until ready to serve.

BISCUITS AND SCONES

Biscuits, scones, soda breads, dumplings, and shortcakes are tender freeform breads, able to hold their own shape.
They are mixed and baked in a very short length of time, a boon to the pioneer baker.

SOURDOUGH SKILLET BISCUITS

These biscuits offer the authentic taste of the old Southwest, and they are easy to make.

MAKES 12 LARGE BISCUITS

2 cups sourdough starter or yogurt starter
2 cups unbleached all-purpose flour
1 tablespoon sugar or honey
1 tablespoon baking powder
¾ teaspoon salt

1] About 2 to 4 hours before baking, let the sourdough starter stand at room temperature. Grease a 12-inch cast-iron skillet. About 1 hour before serving, combine the starter, flour, sugar, baking powder, and salt in a medium bowl. Stir until evenly moistened and the dough clears the sides of the bowl. The dough will be firm and slightly sticky.

2] Pinch off 12 pieces of the soft dough the size of a jumbo egg. Arrange the pieces, with their sides just touching, in the skillet. Let rest at room temperature for about 45 minutes, or until puffy.

3] About 20 minutes before baking, preheat the oven to 400°F.

4] Bake in the center of the oven until the biscuits are dark brown and crusty, 25 to 30 minutes. Cool for 5 minutes before serving hot.

VARIATIONS
Add ½ cup crisp, crumbled bacon or raisins to the dough in Step 1.

Pat 3 tablespoons soft butter in the bottom of the skillet and sprinkle with brown sugar before putting in the biscuits. When the biscuits are turned out of the pan, a caramel syrup will coat each one.

MOUNTAIN COWBOY BROWN BISCUITS

This classic buttermilk biscuit has a ratio of three parts dry ingredients to one part tangy liquid, which creates a dough that bakes high, fluffy, and crisp-crusted. Brown biscuits are traditional Southwest breakfast fare with honey and butter. Day-old biscuits are dunked into coffee.

MAKES 16 LARGE BISCUITS

3 tablespoons *each* flour and cornmeal, mixed,
    for sprinkling
2 cups unbleached all-purpose flour
2 cups whole wheat pastry flour
4 teaspoons baking powder
1 teaspoon baking soda
1 teaspoon salt
12 tablespoons (1½ sticks) unsalted butter, lard,
    or solid vegetable shortening, chilled and
    cut into pieces
1½ cups cold buttermilk

1] Preheat the oven to 425°F. Grease or line a baking sheet with parchment paper and sprinkle with the flour and cornmeal.

2] In a large bowl, combine the all-purpose flour, whole wheat pastry flour, baking powder, baking soda, and salt. Cut the butter into the dry ingredients with a pastry blender or 2 knives until the mixture resembles coarse crumbs, with no large chunks of butter. If the butter gets very soft, refrigerate for 20 minutes. Add the buttermilk, stirring just to moisten all the ingredients. The dough will be moist, then stiffen while stirring. It should be slightly shaggy, but not sticky.

3] Turn the dough out onto a lightly floured work surface and knead gently about 10 times, or just until the dough holds together smoothly. Roll or pat out the dough into a rectangle about 1¼ inches thick. Take care not to add too much flour, or the biscuits will be tough. Cut with a floured knife into 16 equal squares. Place on the baking sheet, no more than ½ inch apart.

4] Bake for 15 to 18 minutes, or until golden brown. Let rest a few minutes and serve hot.

VARIATION
Add 1 cup dried blueberries or chopped pitted dates to the dough in Step 3.

RED PEPPER JELLY SCONES

Colorful pepper jelly sits atop these savory scones. Serve them with lunch or with a glass of wine as an appetizer.

MAKES 12 SCONES

2 cups unbleached all-purpose flour
½ cup finely chopped walnuts or pistachios
2 teaspoons baking powder
½ teaspoon baking soda
¼ teaspoon salt
6 tablespoons (¾ stick) unsalted butter, chilled and
    cut into pieces
⅔ cup buttermilk
⅓ cup homemade Red Pepper Jelly (page 132)
    or store-bought mild or hot pepper jelly

1] Preheat the oven to 400°F. Grease or line a baking sheet with parchment paper.

2] In a medium bowl, combine the flour, nuts, baking powder, baking soda, and salt. Cut in the butter with a fork or a heavy-duty electric mixer until the mixture resembles coarse crumbs. Add the buttermilk to the dry mixture and stir until a sticky dough forms.

3] Turn out the dough onto a lightly floured work surface and knead gently just until the dough holds together, about 8 times. Divide into 2 equal portions and pat each into a 1-inch-thick round about 6 inches in diameter. With a knife or straight edge, cut each round into 6 wedges.

4] Place the scones about 1 inch apart on the baking sheet. With the tip of a sharp knife, make a 1-inch long slit in the center of each triangle. Open each slit slightly into an oval with a small spoon and fill each with a mounded teaspoon of pepper jelly. Bake in the center of the oven until crusty and golden brown, 15 to 20 minutes. Serve warm or at room temperature.

ORANGE-GOAT CHEESE BISCUITS

Soft fresh goat cheese is one of the most versatile of cheeses. It has a tangy, slightly acid flavor and is usually brilliant white in color. When heated, it gets soft rather than stringy. No two goat cheeses taste exactly alike, so the flavor of your biscuits will depend on the cheese you choose. For a taste of New Mexico, use cheese from Coonridge Farms.

MAKES ABOUT FIFTEEN 2-INCH DINNER BISCUITS
OR THIRTY 1¼-INCH COCKTAIL BISCUITS

2 cups unbleached all-purpose flour
2 teaspoons baking powder
½ teaspoon baking soda
¼ teaspoon salt
Grated zest of 1 orange
5 tablespoons unsalted butter, chilled and
    cut into small pieces
¼ pound fresh goat cheese, such as a domestic
    queso fuego, chabis, or French Montrachet
⅓ to ½ cup milk

1] Preheat the oven to 425°F. Grease or line a baking sheet with parchment paper.

2] In a medium bowl, combine all the dry ingredients and the orange zest. Quickly cut in the cold butter with a pastry blender or fingers until the mixture resembles coarse meal. If butter gets soft, refrigerate for about 15 minutes.

3] In a small bowl, combine the goat cheese and ⅓ cup milk, and beat until smooth. Pour into the dry mixture. Stir until evenly moistened and the dough clears the sides of the bowl. Add up to 1 tablespoon more liquid, if the dough seems too crumbly.

4] Scrape the dough out of the bowl onto a lightly floured work surface. Knead gently until the dough just holds together, about 10 times. Pat the dough into 1 thick piece, ¾ to 1 inch thick. Using a 2- to 3-inch cutter dipped in flour to form a round or other desired shape, press firmly in a straight up and down motion to form clean edges as you cut out biscuits. Cut out forms as close together as possible for a minimum of leftover dough. Press scraps gently together for additional biscuits. Arrange the biscuits on the baking sheet, at least ½ inch apart.

5] Bake in the center of the oven until the biscuits begin to brown, 12 to 15 minutes. Cool for 5 minutes before serving.

JALAPEÑO JACK CHEESE SCONES

Use the fiery jalapeño when deep green. These scones are good with a glass of wine for entertaining.

MAKES 24 SCONES

2⅔ cups unbleached all-purpose flour
⅓ cup fine- or medium-grind yellow cornmeal
1¼ cups shredded hot pepper Monterey jack cheese
    or *queso asadero* with jalapeños
1 tablespoon baking powder
½ teaspoon salt
6 tablespoons (¾ stick) unsalted butter, chilled
    and cut into pieces
2 large eggs, beaten
1 cup half-and-half

1] Preheat the oven to 400°F. Grease or line 2 baking sheets with parchment paper.

2] In a medium bowl, combine the flour, cornmeal, cheese, baking powder, and salt. Cut in the butter with a pastry blender or heavy-duty electric mixer until the mixture resembles coarse crumbs. In a small bowl, whisk together the eggs and half-and-half. Add to the dry mixture and stir until a sticky dough forms. Add up to 1 tablespoon extra liquid if the dough is too stiff to mix.

3] Turn the dough out onto a lightly floured work surface. Knead gently about 10 times, just until dough holds together. With a rolling pin, roll out the dough into a ¾-inch-thick circle and cut with a floured 2-inch cutter to make 20 scones. Reroll scraps to cut out additional scones. Place the scones on the prepared baking sheets, about 1 inch apart.

4] Bake until crusty and golden brown, 15 to 20 minutes. Serve immediately.

ACORN-OATMEAL DROP BISCUITS

Acorns from Gambel and Emery oaks, indigenous to the South-west, are a thin-shelled sweet nut that can be eaten straight off the tree. Other varieties need to be leached before roasting and grinding. Acorn meal is very nutty in flavor, blending well with wheat flour and oats. These biscuits would be more authentic if made with bacon fat. If you would like to try it, just substitute the fat for the butter.

MAKES 9 BISCUITS

    1 cup unbleached all-purpose flour
    ½ cup finely ground acorn meal (see page 136)
    ½ cup rolled oats, ground to a coarse meal in the
        food processor, or oat flour
    3 tablespoons sugar
    1 tablespoon baking powder
    ½ teaspoon salt
    ¼ cup (½ stick) cold unsalted butter, cut into pieces
    1 large egg
    ½ cup cold milk, evaporated milk, or light cream

1] Preheat the oven to 400°F. Grease or line a baking sheet with parchment paper.

2] In a mixing bowl, combine the flour, acorn meal, ground oats, sugar, baking powder, and salt. Cut the butter into the dry ingredients with a pastry blender or 2 knives until the mixture resembles coarse meal with small chunks of butter. Combine the egg and milk in a measuring cup. Add to the dry ingredients, stirring just until moistened. The dough will cling to the sides of the bowl. Add additional milk or cream 1 tablespoon at a time if the mixture seems too dry. Using a large spoon, drop spoonfuls of the dough, about ¼ cup each, onto the prepared baking sheet, about 1 inch apart.

3] Bake in the center of the oven until the tops are brown and firm to the touch, 18 to 22 minutes. Serve warm.

BAKING POWDER CORN BREADS

Cakelike baking powder corn bread is prepared in all areas and kitchens of the Southwest.
Its simplicity of flavor allows for infinite variations—from using all the colors of cornmeal to adding
chilies, cheeses, nuts, and fruits.

BLUE CORN BREAD

Here is a good corn bread that is not sweet, yet still moist and full of flavor. For a rustic container, use this technique, once common in Native kitchens: Line the greased baking pan with a layer of corn husks, leaving about three inches standing up above the sides of the pan. Turn the baked bread out of the pan in its own wrapping. For an authentic touch, add a scant tablespoon of culinary ash (see page 18) to the batter; it will enhance the blue color. Red or yellow cornmeal can be substituted for the blue.

MAKES ONE 9-INCH ROUND BREAD

1 cup unbleached all-purpose flour
1 cup fine-grind blue cornmeal, or *harina para atole*
2 teaspoons baking powder
½ teaspoon baking soda
½ teaspoon salt
1¼ cups sour cream or *Crema Mexicana* (see page 139)
¼ cup corn oil
2 large eggs

1] Preheat the oven to 375°F. Grease a 9-inch springform pan or pie plate.

2] In a medium bowl, combine the flour, cornmeal, baking powder, baking soda, and salt. In another bowl, whisk together the sour cream, oil, and eggs. Add to the dry ingredients and stir with a spoon or rubber spatula until the ingredients are just blended. The batter will be very thick. Take care not to overmix. Spoon the batter into the pan.

3] Bake for 25 to 30 minutes, or until it is golden around the edges and the top is dry and springy to the touch. A cake tester inserted into the center will come out clean. Let stand in the pan for 15 minutes before cutting into wedges to serve.

VARIATION
Cherry Blue Corn Bread: Gently fold in 1 can (16 ounces) drained pitted sour pie cherries or 1¼ cups prepared sweetened chokecherries into the batter in Step 2.

PREPARING FRESH CHOKECHERRIES FOR BAKING

Combine 1½ cups fresh whole chokecherries and ¼ cup sugar in a small nonreactive saucepan and cover with 2 cups of water. Bring to a boil, reduce the heat, and simmer for 20 minutes. Drain. Squeeze the cherries to remove the pits.

CHIPOTLE CORN BREAD

Chipotles are smoked and dried jalapeños; they are readily available canned. This corn bread is best baked in a cast-iron skillet, the quintessential Southwestern cooking pan, but you can use a springform or pie pan.

MAKES ONE 10-INCH ROUND BREAD

1 cup unbleached all-purpose flour
1¼ cups coarse-grind yellow cornmeal, or
   masa harina para tamales
1 tablespoon sugar
1½ teaspoons baking powder
½ teaspoon salt
1¼ cups buttermilk
2 eggs
⅓ cup corn oil
2 canned whole chipotles in adobo
1 cup shredded Monterey jack cheese

1] Preheat the oven to 400°F. Grease a cast-iron skillet and place it in the oven. Or grease a 10-inch springform or pie plate and set aside.

2] In a large bowl, combine the flour, cornmeal, sugar, baking powder, and salt. In a food processor or blender, combine the buttermilk, eggs, oil, and chipotles. Blend until the chipotles are finely chopped. Add the buttermilk mixture and the cheese to the dry ingredients and stir with a spoon or rubber spatula until ingredients are just blended. Take care not to overmix. Pour the batter into the skillet or pan.

3] Bake for 20 to 25 minutes, or until golden around the edges. A cake tester inserted into the center will come out clean. Let stand for 15 minutes before cutting into wedges to serve.

BLUE CORN BREAD WITH PECANS AND CHEDDAR

Longhorn cheddar, a tall, rindless cylinder, bright orange in color, is very popular in Southwest cooking. It is a great melting cheese that complements buttery Texas pecans, chiles, and olives as well as melting into bread with streaks of bright flavor.

MAKES ONE 9-INCH ROUND BREAD

¼ cup pecans
1½ cups fine-grind blue cornmeal or *harina para atole*
1½ cups unbleached all-purpose flour
¼ cup sugar
1 tablespoon chili powder, preferably homemade
   (see page 138)
1 tablespoon baking powder
½ teaspoon baking soda
1 teaspoon salt
1 cup shredded Longhorn cheddar
½ cup minced red bell pepper
3 large eggs
1¼ cups buttermilk
6 tablespoons (¾ stick) unsalted butter or lard, melted

1] Preheat the oven to 375°F. Grease a 9-inch springform pan or deep cake pan.

2] In a blender or food processor, grind the pecans and 1 cup of the cornmeal to the consistency of a fine meal. In a large bowl, combine the pecan meal, the remaining ½ cup cornmeal, flour, sugar, chili powder, baking powder, baking soda, and salt. Add the cheese and bell pepper. Toss to evenly distribute. In another bowl, mix the eggs, buttermilk, and butter. Add to the dry ingredients and stir until all the ingredients are just blended. Take care not to overmix. Pour the batter into the pan.

3] Bake for 30 to 35 minutes, or until it is golden brown around the edges and a cake tester comes out clean. Let stand for 15 minutes before cutting into wedges to serve.

BACON BLUE CORN STICKS

Although any baking powder corn bread recipe can be used to make corncob-shape sticks, this recipe reigns supreme. The cast-iron pans, relatives of the ceramic molds used by the Aztecs to shape clay corn ears, are sold in specialty food stores. When the sticks were made by the Spanish settlers in tiny individual oblong pans, they were called jalapeños. This bread may also be made in an 8-inch square or 14-by-9-inch oblong pan and cut into squares to serve. A shell-shaped French madeleine pan makes nice individual hors d'oeuvre bites.

MAKES 28 STICKS

1 cup fine-grind blue cornmeal, or *harina para atole*
1 cup unbleached all-purpose flour
1 tablespoon baking powder
1 teaspoon salt
½ cup (tightly packed) finely chopped fried bacon,
    at room temperature
1 cup sautéed red and green peppers or
    fresh corn kernels
1¼ cups plain yogurt
2 large eggs, separated
2 tablespoons honey, warmed for easy pouring
½ cup (1 stick) unsalted butter, melted

1] Preheat the oven to 450°F. Place 4 cast-iron corncob pans in the oven to heat while mixing the batter.

2] In a large bowl, combine the cornmeal, flour, baking powder, and salt. Stir in the bacon and peppers. In another bowl, whisk together the yogurt, egg yolks, honey, and melted butter just until blended. Add the liquid mixture to the dry ingredients and stir with a large spoon or rubber spatula until all ingredients are just blended.

3] In a clean bowl, beat the egg whites until soft peaks form. Fold into the batter just until no white streaks remain. Take care not to overmix.

4] Using thick oven mitts, carefully remove the hot pans from the oven and brush with melted butter or vegetable shortening or spray with vegetable oil spray (my preference). Fill each mold half to two-thirds full with the batter. Immediately return the pans to the oven and bake 15 to 20 minutes, or until puffed in the center and golden brown. A cake tester inserted into the center will come out clean. Let stand for 5 minutes in the pan before turning out onto a wire rack to cool. Serve warm.

MUFFINS

*Muffins are one of the best ways for a baker to showcase the ingredients of the Southwest.
The following muffin recipes are designed to be baked in a standard muffin pan with 2¾-inch cups in sets
of six and twelve, but the batter can be used to make twice the number of mini muffins
or half the number of jumbo muffins.*

BLUEBERRY–BLUE CORN MUFFINS

*Banana gives this berry corn muffin a unique flavor. Fresh
raspberries, boysenberries, even tart wild berries, such as buffalo
berries or blackberries or mesa-grown wolf berries (sacred to the
Hopi and known as* kevepsi), *as well as blueberries work. You
can also use frozen berries for this. After adding the berries to the
batter, mix as little as possible to avoid breaking up the berries
and giving the baked muffin a streaky look.*

MAKES 16 MUFFINS

1¼ cups whole wheat pastry flour
1 cup unbleached all-purpose flour
¾ cup fine-grind blue cornmeal, or *harina para atole*
¾ cup (packed) light brown sugar
1 tablespoon baking powder
1 teaspoon baking soda
½ teaspoon salt
1½ cups buttermilk
⅓ cup corn oil
1 small to medium banana, mashed
1 teaspoon pure vanilla extract
3 large eggs
2 cups fresh or unthawed frozen whole blueberries

1] Preheat the oven to 375°F. Grease the cups of 2 or
3 standard muffin tins.

2] In a medium bowl, combine the whole wheat and all-
purpose flours, the cornmeal, brown sugar, baking powder,
baking soda, and salt. In another bowl, combine the buttermilk, oil, mashed banana, vanilla, and eggs with a whisk.
Add to the dry ingredients, stirring just until moistened; the
batter will be lumpy. Do not overmix. Gently fold the blueberries in with a large spatula to distribute evenly. Spoon
the batter into muffin cups, filling sixteen of the cups level
with the top.

3] Bake for 25 to 30 minutes, or until golden and the tops
are dry and springy to the touch. A cake tester inserted
into the center will come out clean. Cool in the pan for 5
minutes before removing to cool on a rack. Serve warm.

BLUE OR RED CORN MUFFINS

Blue cornmeal will give you muffins that are a gentle lavender; red cornmeal will give you a delicate pink color.

MAKES 8 MUFFINS

1 cup fine-grind blue or red cornmeal, or
   harina para atole
1 cup unbleached all-purpose flour
3 tablespoons light brown sugar
1 teaspoon baking powder
1 teaspoon baking soda
½ teaspoon salt
1¼ cups buttermilk or ½ cup dried buttermilk
   powder and 1¼ cups water
¼ cup corn or olive oil
1 large egg

1] Preheat the oven to 375°F. Grease the cups of 2 standard muffin tins.

2] In a medium bowl, combine the cornmeal, flour, brown sugar, baking powder, baking soda, and salt. In another bowl, whisk together the buttermilk, oil, and egg. Add to the dry ingredients, stirring just until moistened. Spoon the batter into the muffin tins, filling eight of the cups level with the top.

3] Bake for about 20 minutes, or until golden and the tops are dry and firm to the touch. A cake tester inserted into the center will come out clean. Cool in the pan for 5 minutes before removing to cool on a rack. Serve warm.

VARIATIONS

Increase the brown sugar to ¾ cup and fold 1½ cups chopped fresh strawberries into the batter in Step 2.

Fold 1 cup cooked black beans, patted dry, or chopped roasted red peppers into the batter in Step 2.

Substitute maple syrup for brown sugar.

SANTA FE BLUE CORN MUFFINS

Jacquie McMahan adapted these muffins, which she learned to make at the Santa Fe School of Cooking, which learned them from Chef Kip McClerin during his stint at La Casa Sena restaurant in Santa Fe. The chef would probably be surprised at how far his recipe has traveled! I love these muffins so much that I had to include my own version.

MAKES 12 MUFFINS

½ cup (1 stick) unsalted butter or margarine,
   at room temperature
½ cup sugar
5 large eggs
½ cup milk
1 can (4 ounces) canned green chiles, diced
1 cup blanched fresh or thawed frozen white
   corn kernels
1 cup coarsely shredded Longhorn or
   Colby cheddar cheese
1 cup coarsely shredded Monterey jack cheese
1 cup unbleached all-purpose flour
1¼ cups fine-grind blue cornmeal or *harina para atole*
2 teaspoons baking powder
½ teaspoon salt

121

1] Preheat the oven to 375°F. Grease the cups of 2 standard muffin tins.

2] In medium bowl, cream the butter and sugar until fluffy. Add the eggs, milk, and chiles, beating until well blended. In another bowl, combine the corn, cheeses, flour, corn-meal, baking powder, and salt. Add the corn-flour mixture to the butter mixture, stirring in an additional ¼ cup flour if the batter is too loose. Beat well to make a thick, creamy batter that falls off the spoon in clumps. Spoon the batter into the muffin tins, filling each cup level with the top.

3] Bake in the oven for 20 to 25 minutes, or until golden and the tops are dry and springy to the touch. A cake tester inserted into the center will come out clean. Cool in the pan for 5 minutes before removing to cool on a rack. Serve warm or store in the refrigerator.

QUINOA WHOLE WHEAT MUFFINS

Quinoa, the sacred grain of the Incas, is now being grown in the mountains of Colorado and New Mexico. This millet-sized grain has a delicate sweet flavor.

MAKES 10 MUFFINS

    1 cup whole wheat flour
    ½ cup unbleached all-purpose flour
    ¼ cup (packed) light brown sugar or ½ cone
        piloncillo, crumbled
    1½ teaspoons baking powder
    1½ teaspoons baking soda
    ½ teaspoon salt
    1 cup buttermilk
    2 large eggs
    3 tablespoons sunflower seed oil or other vegetable oil

    1¼ cups cooked quinoa
    ½ cup sunflower seeds

1] Preheat the oven to 375°F. Grease the cups of 2 standard muffin tins.

2] In a medium bowl, combine the flours, brown sugar, baking powder, baking soda, and salt. In another bowl, whisk together the buttermilk, eggs, and oil. Add the quinoa and sunflower seeds. Add to the dry ingredients, stirring just until moistened. Spoon the batter into 10 of the muffin cups, filling each cup level with the top.

3] Bake for 20 to 25 minutes, or until golden and the tops are dry and springy to the touch. A cake tester inserted into the center will come out clean. Cool in the pan 5 minutes before removing to cool on a rack. Serve warm.

COOKING QUINOA
Makes about 1¼ cups

    1 cup water
    ½ cup quinoa, well rinsed

In a small saucepan over high heat, bring the water to a rolling boil. Add the quinoa and reduce the heat as low as possible. Cover and cook until the water is absorbed and the quinoa is tender, about 15 minutes. Let stand off the heat for 10 minutes. Set aside to cool. (Quinoa may be refrigerated overnight.)

QUICK LOAVES

*Quick breads all use a chemical leavener, such as baking powder, baking soda, or cream of tartar,
besides the mechanical action of creaming or beating in plenty of air, to lighten the batter.
Early bakers used* tequesquite *(also known as* texquite), *ground pumice rock containing sodium nitrate,
a forerunner of saleratus or baking soda. All-purpose flour is best, rather than bread flours,
since the chemical leaveners produce the necessary quick rise.*

PUMPKIN-APPLE BREAD

*This is one of my favorite quick breads: dense, moist, and flecked
with spices and bits of apple. Desert apples come to harvest during
the summer months; they are smaller and sweeter than commercial
varieties, due to dry farming techniques. Any firm cooking apple
will work.*

MAKES TWO 9-BY-5-INCH
OR SIX 6-BY-4-INCH LOAVES

3 cups unbleached all-purpose flour

2 teaspoons baking soda

2 teaspoons ground cinnamon

1 teaspoon *each* freshly grated nutmeg, ground cloves,
   and ground allspice

1 teaspoon salt

2 cups sugar

4 large eggs

2 cups canned or homemade pumpkin puree
   (page 141)

¾ cup vegetable or sunflower seed oil

1½ teaspoons pure vanilla extract

2 cups peeled, cored, and finely chopped firm apples
   (3 medium apples)

Spice Crumbs

¾ cup sugar

3 tablespoons unbleached all-purpose flour

2 teaspoons ground cinnamon

Pinch *each* of grated nutmeg, ground cloves, and
   ground allspice

3 tablespoons unsalted butter, at room temperature,
   cut into small pieces

1] Preheat the oven to 350°F. Grease two 9-by-5-inch or
six 6-by-4-inch loaf pans.

2] In a medium bowl, combine the flour, baking soda,
spices, and salt. In another bowl, with a whisk or an electric
mixer, beat together the sugar, eggs, pumpkin puree, and oil
until light and fluffy, about 2 minutes. Add the vanilla.

3] Add the flour mixture to the sugar mixture and beat just
until smooth. Do not overmix. With a large spatula, fold in
the apples. Scrape the batter into the pans.

4] *To prepare the spice crumbs:* In a medium bowl,
combine the sugar, flour, and spices. Work in the butter
until crumbly. Sprinkle each loaf with spice crumbs.

5] Bake in the center of the oven for 50 to 60 minutes, or
until the top is firm, the loaf pulls away from the sides of
the pans, and a cake tester inserted into the center comes
out clean. Remove from the pans to a wire rack to cool
completely. When cooled, wrap in plastic wrap and let
stand at room temperature until serving.

SAGUARO CACTUS BREAD

The Tohono O'odham Indians of southern Arizona built their homes in saguaro forests that were hundreds of years old. They celebrated the New Year at the summer harvest. Traditional saguaro bread recipes call for a mixture of ground saguaro seeds, sunflower seeds, and cornmeal moistened with saguaro pulp and water and baked on corn husks in a pit. These days, saguaro puree can be used in quick breads just like applesauce. This recipe is adapted from The Tumbleweed Gourmet by Carolyn J. Niethammer (University of Arizona Press, 1987).

MAKES ONE 8½-BY-4½-INCH LOAF

1¾ cups unbleached all-purpose flour
½ teaspoon baking soda
¼ teaspoon cream of tartar
½ teaspoon salt
½ cup (1 stick) unsalted butter, room temperature
½ cup sugar
2 large eggs
1½ teaspoons pure vanilla extract
½ cup plain yogurt or sour cream
1 cup saguaro puree, fresh or frozen and thawed
  (page 142)

1] Preheat the oven to 350°F. Grease an 8½-by-4½-inch loaf pan.

2] In a medium bowl, combine the flour, baking soda, cream of tartar, and salt. In another bowl, cream the butter and sugar until light and fluffy, about 2 minutes. Add the eggs, vanilla, yogurt, and saguaro puree. Beat just until smooth. Add the flour mixture to the butter mixture and beat just until smooth. Do not overmix. Scrape the batter into the pan.

3] Bake in the center of the oven for 45 to 50 minutes, or until the top is firm, the loaf pulls away from the sides of the pan, and a cake tester inserted into the center comes out clean. Remove from the pan to a wire rack to cool completely. When cooled, wrap in plastic wrap and let stand at room temperature until serving.

MANGO BREAD

Mangoes from Mexico hit the market during the summer months, and this bread is an unusual way to use them. They should be ripe but not too tender, so that the flesh holds its shape during baking. Since the pit is stubbornly clingstone, cut the fruit into three sections, leaving the pit in one section, and slip a paring knife under the skin to peel it off. This loaf can be dressed up with Fresh Lime Glaze (page 128) for special occasions.

MAKES TWO 7-BY-3-INCH LOAVES

2 cups unbleached all-purpose flour

2 teaspoons ground cinnamon

2 teaspoons baking soda

½ teaspoon salt

½ cup dried cherries or raisins, plumped in hot
water for 10 minutes and drained

1 cup sugar

2 large eggs

1 teaspoon pure vanilla extract

2½ cups chopped firm-ripe mangoes
(about 3½ pounds)

1 tablespoon fresh lemon or lime juice

1] Preheat the oven to 350°F. Grease two 7-by-3-inch loaf pans (I use disposable aluminum).

2] In a medium bowl, combine the flour, cinnamon, baking soda, and salt. Add the dried cherries and stir until evenly distributed. In another bowl, with a whisk or an electric mixer, beat together the sugar, eggs, and oil until fluffy and light colored, about 3 minutes. Add the vanilla. Add the flour mixture to the sugar mixture and beat just until smooth. Do not overmix. With a large spatula, fold in the mangoes and lemon juice. Scrape the batter into the pans.

3] Bake in the center of the oven for 35 to 40 minutes, or until the top is firm, the loaf pulls away from the sides of the pans, and a cake tester inserted into the center comes out clean. Remove from the pans to a wire rack to cool completely. When cooled, wrap in plastic wrap and let stand at room temperature until serving.

PAN DE LOS TRES REYES

This is the quick bread version of the yeasted Three Kings Bread Ring (page 65) served on January 6 for El Día de los Tres Reyes Magos. *Bake it in a fluted ring mold (I use one that fits into my springform pan) and fill the center with winter greenery and a white candle to represent the Christ Child. Stand three colored tapers—brown, black, and yellow—in the cake to represent the three kings. Remember that the person getting the slice with the figurine is especially blessed and will reign as king or queen during the festivities.*

MAKES ONE 9-INCH ROUND LOAF

3 cups unbleached all-purpose flour
Grated zest of 1 orange
2 teaspoons ground cinnamon
Pinch of ground allspice
2 teaspoons baking powder
½ teaspoon salt
¾ cup golden raisins
½ cup dried currants
¼ cup diced dried pineapple
¼ cup diced dried papaya
¼ cup slivered blanched almonds
1 cup (2 sticks) unsalted butter, at room temperature
¾ cup sugar
3 large eggs
⅓ cup milk
1 figurine, whole almond, or large dried bean

1] Preheat the oven to 350°F. Grease a 9-inch fluted ring mold.

2] In a medium bowl, combine the flour, orange zest, cinnamon, allspice, baking powder, and salt. Add the raisins, currants, pineapple, papaya, and almonds. Stir to distribute. In another bowl, cream the butter and sugar until light and fluffy, about 2 minutes. Add the eggs and milk and beat until smooth.

3] Add the flour mixture to the butter mixture in 3 additions, beating until just smooth. Do not overmix. Scrape the batter into the pan. Press the figurine into the center of the batter.

4] Bake in the center of the oven for 50 to 60 minutes, or until the top is firm, the loaf pulls away from the sides of the pan, and a cake tester inserted into the center comes out clean. Let stand for 15 minutes before turning the bread out onto a rack to cool, right side up. When cooled, wrap in plastic wrap and let stand at room temperature until serving. It is best served the day it is baked.

GLAZES

Completely optional, a glaze is brushed on the surface of an unbaked loaf to give a deep sheen or finishing touch.
Most country-style breads look quite complete with their natural matte finish, or with just a sprinkling of seeds or whole
grains to reflect the ingredients inside, or with a dusting of flour for an earthy look.
An egg wash is used to produce a shiny crust, as well as to act as a glue for nuts, seeds, herbs, grain flakes,
and decorations made out of dough. Because they are high in protein, the yolk with milk or cream produces a dark crust;
such glazes are often used on sweet breads rich in fat and sugar. Egg white with water makes a shiny finish for a lean dough,
such as a French-style bread. Fats—lard, melted butter or margarine, or oils—can be brushed on a loaf at any point before,
during, or after baking to keep the crust soft and shiny. Infusing the oil with fresh herbs, dried chiles, or garlic gives
an added dimension to the flavor. The glaze and embellishments should complement the flavors of the loaf.

EGG GLAZE
1 egg white
1 tablespoon water
Dash salt

In a small bowl, whisk the ingredients together until combined and foamy.

RICH EGG GLAZE
1 whole egg
1 tablespoon milk or cream

In a small bowl, whisk the ingredients together until combined.

POWDERED SUGAR GLAZE
This powdered sugar glaze, azúcar glas, also known as a confitura in Mexican baking, is for fresh-baked sweet breads and rolls. Top the loaf with dried or candied fruit, seeds, or whole and/or chopped nuts while the icing is moist. As the glaze sets up and dries, they will stay in place. Add an extra ¼ to ½ cup of sugar for a spreadable icing. Adding a bit of condensed milk, a tip from Jacquie McMahan, balances the flavor and smoothes the texture of the sugar.

1 cup sifted powdered sugar
1 tablespoon unsalted butter, melted
1 tablespoon sweetened condensed skim milk
2 to 3 tablespoons hot milk or cream, spirit or liqueur, or hot water

In a small bowl, combine all of the ingredients and whisk until smooth. Adjust the consistency by adding more hot milk, a few drops at a time. Drizzle over warm or cool bread or sweet rolls.

VARIATIONS
Vanilla: Add ½ teaspoon pure vanilla extract.
Almond: Add ½ teaspoon almond extract.
Anise: Add ½ teaspoon anise extract.
Citrus: Substitute fresh or thawed frozen concentrated lemon, orange, lime, or tangerine juice for the milk.
Dark Chocolate: Add 1 tablespoon unsweetened cocoa.
White Chocolate: Add 1 ounce white chocolate chips to the hot milk before mixing.
Coconut: Substitute thawed frozen or canned cream of coconut for the milk.
Coffee: Add 1 teaspoon powdered instant espresso.
Spice: Add ½ teaspoon ground cinnamon, coriander, or nutmeg.

Saffron: Add a small pinch of saffron or *azafrán* powder or threads to the hot liquid. Let stand 10 minutes to meld flavors. Rewarm before mixing, if necessary.

Liqueur: Substitute a liqueur for the milk, such as Tia Maria, Kahlúa, rum, crème de banana, curaçao, Triple Sec, Grand Passion, Mandarine Napoléon, peach brandy, crème de cacao, Rompopo, Almendrado, or Amaretto.

HONEY GLAZE

Good as a glossy finish on sweet breads. Brush it over the bread while hot.

- 2 tablespoons honey
- 2 tablespoons very hot water
- 2 tablespoons powdered sugar
- 1 teaspoon all-purpose flour

In a small bowl, combine the honey and hot water. Add the sugar and flour and whisk the ingredients together until smooth.

BROWN SUGAR GLAZE

Good on hearty whole-grain breads, sweet breads, and rolls. Brush loaves twice with the warm glaze, once during baking and once at the end.

- ½ cup (packed) dark brown sugar or 1 cone *piloncillo,* crumbled
- 3 tablespoons hot water
- 3 tablespoons cream sherry

In a small saucepan, combine the brown sugar and water. Bring to a boil and boil 1 minute to dissolve the sugar before removing from the heat. Add the sherry.

GARLIC OR CHILE OIL WASH

Good on savory breads.

- 1 tablespoon unsalted butter
- 1 tablespoon olive oil
- 1 garlic clove or small dried chile, crushed

In a small saucepan, combine the butter and oil. Gently heat on low just to melt the butter. Remove from the heat. Add the garlic and let the mixture come to room temperature. Brush on loaves just before baking.

FRESH LIME GLAZE

Drizzle over plain or nut-filled sweet breads or rolls.

- 1 cup sifted powdered sugar
- 1 tablespoon unsalted butter, melted
- Grated zest of 1 lime
- 2 to 3 tablespoons fresh lime juice

In a small bowl, combine the ingredients and whisk until smooth. Adjust the consistency by adding more juice a few drops at a time.

CHEESE SPREADS AND BUTTERS

Goat cheese and compound butters combine herbs, citrus rinds, honey, chiles, and fruit to create a wide variety of sweet and savory spreads. Use as you would a plain butter on fresh bread, toast, muffins, and other quick breads.

FRESH GOAT CHEESE

Goat's milk cheese, queso de cabra, *was made in the earliest Spanish settlements. When you discover how simple it is to make your own, you'll be inspired to give this recipe a try. Rennet tablets are available in supermarkets and fresh goat's milk in natural food stores. Get the milk as fresh as possible, as the flavor changes as it ages. Do not use ultra-pasteurized milk; it will not coagulate properly. Serve the cheese with hot tortillas, crusty breads, or formed into a mound with apple butter or red pepper jelly poured over for spreading. Makes about 1 pound.*

2 quarts fresh whole goat's milk
4 rennet tablets
2 tablespoons water
½ teaspoon salt

1] In a heavy saucepan, heat the milk to exactly 110°F. on an instant-read or other accurate kitchen thermometer. If the milk is too hot, let stand until the proper temperature. In a small bowl, crush the rennet tablets and add the water. Add to the warm milk and stir immediately. Let the pan stand at room temperature (about 75°F.) for 20 minutes until the milk is like custard.

2] Line a colander with 2 layers of clean cheesecloth and set over a deep bowl to catch the whey. With a large spoon, transfer the curds into the colander. Stir in the salt and cover lightly with plastic wrap. Let stand at room temperature for 8 hours to overnight; the longer it stands, the firmer the cheese. Pull up the ends of the cheesecloth and form the cheese into a ball. Or mold it into a shape for entertaining. Discard the whey or use it in bread recipes.

(The cheese may be stored in the refrigerator, covered with plastic wrap, for up to 1 week.)

SWEET VANILLA GOAT CHEESE

Vanilla, along with cinnamon, is the most common spice flavoring used in Mexican baking. Makes about 1 cup.

8 ounces (1 cup) fresh goat cheese, domestic chabis, or French Montrachet
3 tablespoons powdered sugar
2 teaspoons pure vanilla extract

With an electric mixer or in a food processor, blend all the ingredients just until smooth and fluffy. Scrape down the sides as needed. (May be stored, covered, in the refrigerator for up to 1 week.)

GOAT CHEESE SPREAD WITH CHIPOTLES

This spread is good with fresh corn tortillas or toasted adobe oven breads. Makes about 2 cups.

1 small shallot, minced
1 to 2 tablespoons minced canned chipotles in adobo, to taste, not drained
8 ounces fresh natural cream cheese, at room temperature
8 ounces fresh goat cheese, domestic chabis, or French Montrachet

In a food processor, mince the shallot and chiles. Add the cheeses and blend just until smooth. Scrape into a small crock or bowl lined with 2 layers of damp cheesecloth. Pack down and fold the edges of the cheesecloth over the top to cover completely. Cover with plastic wrap. To serve, remove the cheese from the mold and place on a serving plate. Remove the cheesecloth. (Cheese may be stored in the refrigerator wrapped in plastic wrap, for up to 2 days.)

SAGE CHEESE WITH PINE NUTS

Sage is a common Southwest herb used as a seasoning as well as for medicinal and religious purposes. The oils can be quite strong, so use fresh sage leaves in moderation in this spread. It improves in flavor when refrigerated overnight. Makes 2 cups.

   8 ounces fresh natural cream cheese,
       at room temperature
   8 ounces fresh goat cheese, domestic chabis,
       or French Montrachet
   ½ cup (1 stick) unsalted butter, at room temperature
   ½ teaspoon white pepper
   1 to 2 tablespoons chopped fresh sage leaves
   1 cup pine nuts, toasted

In a food processor, blend the cheeses, butter, and white pepper until smooth. Add the sage leaves and pine nuts. Process until the nuts are chopped coarse. Scrape into a container. Cover and refrigerate overnight. (Cheese may be stored, well wrapped, in the refrigerator for up to 5 days.)

HONEY BUTTER

This is the butter to serve with hot sopaipillas, biscuits, or melted on waffles. It is wonderful on toast. Makes about 1¾ cups.
   1 cup (2 sticks) unsalted butter at room temperature
   ¾ cup honey, preferably an aromatic cactus honey

Beat the butter until creamy. Add the honey and beat just until combined. Store, covered, in the refrigerator until ready to use. Let stand for 30 minutes at room temperature to soften before serving.

HONEY-LIME BUTTER

Use raw, unfiltered honey and small Mexican key limes, when available. This butter can also be made with grapefruit, lemon, or orange, all popular in the Southwest kitchen. Makes 1 cup.

   ½ cup (1 stick) unsalted butter, at room
       temperature, cut into pieces
   ¼ cup honey, preferably an aromatic cactus honey
   3 tablespoons fresh lime juice
   Grated zest of 1 lime

With an electric mixer or in a food processor, blend the butter, honey, lime juice, and zest just until smooth. Scrape down the sides as needed. Use at room temperature. (The butter may be stored, covered, in the refrigerator for up to 1 week.)

APRICOT BUTTER

Pueblo bakers make a variety of fruit mashes to serve with Indian breads. This recipe may also be made with dried peaches or dried pears. Makes about 1 cup.

   ¼ pound (about 16) dried apricot halves
   ½ cup (1 stick) unsalted butter, at room temperature

In a small saucepan, cover the apricots with water. Bring to a boil and boil for 1 minute. Remove from the heat and let stand for 15 minutes, uncovered. Drain and pat dry. Combine the apricots and butter in a food processor and puree just until combined and smooth. Scrape into a decorative bowl, cover, and refrigerate. Let stand for 15 minutes at room temperature to soften before serving.

SWEET WILD MINT BUTTER

Strip wild spearmint leaves from their stems to make this fresh-tasting butter. Or substitute mint from your garden. Makes ½ cup.

½ cup (1 stick) unsalted butter, at room temperature
3 tablespoons fresh wild spearmint
2 tablespoons powdered sugar
Grated zest of ½ lemon

With an electric mixer or in a food processor, blend all the ingredients just until smooth. Scrape down the sides as needed. Use at room temperature. (The butter may be stored, covered, in the refrigerator for up to 1 week.)

MANGO CURD

Produced by one of the most productive trees in the tropics, fragrant mangoes made into jams and spreads are common in tropical zones. Makes about 2 cups.

4 tablespoons (½ stick) unsalted butter
2 medium-size ripe mangoes (about 1¾ pounds)
½ cup sugar
2 tablespoons fresh lemon juice
Grated zest of 1 lemon
4 large eggs

Melt the butter in the top of a double boiler. Peel and cube the mangos. Puree in a blender or food processor until smooth to make 1 cup puree. Return the puree to the processor and combine with the sugar, lemon juice, zest, and eggs or beat hard with a whisk. It is important that the eggs be beaten well. With the water at a simmer, slowly add the mango-egg mixture to the butter, stirring constantly with a whisk. Cook over medium heat until thickened, about 10 minutes. Pour into a jar and let cool. (Mango curd may be stored, covered, in the refrigerator for up to 1 week.)

CAJETA SPREAD

Cajeta is a traditional Mexican caramel spread made from goat's milk. Makes about 2 cups.

2 cups canned evaporated goat's milk
2 cups cow's milk
1 tablespoon cornstarch
⅛ teaspoon baking soda
1 teaspoon pure vanilla extract
1¼ cups sugar
2 tablespoons light corn syrup
¼ cup water

1] Combine the canned goat's milk and the cow's milk. In a medium saucepan, scald 3 cups of the milk. Pour the remaining 1 cup of milk into a 2-cup measure. Whisk in the cornstarch, baking soda, and vanilla, and set aside.

2] In a large heavy skillet, combine the sugar, corn syrup, and water. Melt over medium heat, stirring constantly with a wooden spoon, until it forms a golden brown caramel liquid. Remove from the heat and let cool for 5 minutes. Slowly and very carefully pour the hot milk into the caramel, taking care if the mixture bubbles up. Add the reserved cup of milk, stirring constantly with a whisk.

3] Return the caramel milk to the heat and bring to a boil. Reduce the heat to medium-low and simmer, uncovered, until very thick and dark brown, stirring occasionally to prevent sticking, 50 to 60 minutes. Remove from the heat and let cool. (Cajeta may be stored in a covered jar in the refrigerator for up to 3 weeks.)

PRESERVES AND HONEYS

Make these preserves in small batches and keep them in the refrigerator,
and you won't have to sterilize the jars and process them in a hot-water bath.

DRIED APPLE BUTTER

Dried apples were a mainstay of Pueblo and Spanish kitchens
for use during the winter months. New Mexico's Chimayo apples
are grown between Taos and Santa Fe in the Sangre de Cristo
Mountains, and the Mimbres and Ruidoso valley varieties farther
south. A fruit butter such as this would be served with warm fresh
cheese curds and atole (see page 20) made with ewe's or goat's milk
steeped with aniseed and honey. Makes about 2 cups.

3 cups dried unsulfured sliced apples
2 cups unsweetened apple juice or cider
2 teaspoons ground cinnamon
1 teaspoon ground allspice
½ teaspoon ground cloves
2 tablespoons unsalted butter

Combine all the ingredients in a heavy saucepan and bring
to a boil. Reduce the heat to a simmer and cook, uncovered, for 30 minutes, stirring occasionally. Remove from
the heat, stir in the butter, and let cool. Puree the apple
butter in a blender or food processor until smooth. Scrape
into a covered jar, cover and refrigerate. (Apple butter may
be stored in the refrigerator for up to 2 months.)

RED PEPPER JELLY

Translucent red and green jellies made from peppers and chiles
are very popular in the Southwest. Ranging in flavor from sweet
to hot and tangy, they are good served with fresh goat or cream
cheeses. Makes about 4 cups.

6 red bell peppers, cut quartered and seeded
1½ teaspoons salt
1 cup champagne vinegar or white wine vinegar
1½ cups sugar

1] Chop the peppers coarsely in a food processor and pour
into a bowl of water. Let stand for 15 minutes. Drain and
sprinkle with salt. Let stand at room temperature for at least
5 hours to overnight.

2] In a large saucepan, combine the vinegar and sugar.
Bring to a boil. Add the peppers. Cook over low heat,
uncovered, for about 1 hour, or until the consistency of
a thin marmalade. Pour into clean jars and let cool to
room temperature. Cover and refrigerate. (Pepper jelly
may be stored in the refrigerator for up to 1 month.)

CHOKECHERRY JELLY

Chokecherries, astringent when raw, cook up into exceptional syrups, jellies, and preserves. Try this on slices of toasted day-old Indian Adobe Oven Bread (page 45). Makes about 5 cups.

3½ pounds ripe chokecherries
1 teaspoon almond extract
6 cups sugar
1 bottle (3 ounces) liquid pectin

1] Wash, stem, and pit the chokecherries. Place in a deep large saucepan and add 3 cups of water. Bring to a boil. Reduce the heat and simmer, covered, for 20 minutes. Set aside to cool for 1 hour.

2] Pour into a damp cloth jelly bag or a strainer lined with 4 thicknesses of cheesecloth set over a bowl and let drain 30 minutes. Squeeze or press the bag to extract any remaining juice. You should have about 3 cups of juice.

3] Place the juice in a large saucepan and add the almond extract and sugar. Bring to a boil over high heat. Stirring constantly, add the pectin. Bring back to a boil and boil hard for 1 minute, stirring constantly. Remove from the heat, skim off foam with a metal spoon, and pour into clean glass jars. Let cool to room temperature. Cover and refrigerate. (The jelly may be stored in the refrigerator for up to 6 months.)

MARGARITA JELLY

This recipe, adapted from one developed by Sure-Jell, makes an excellent spread for biscuits. The alcohol in the liquors will evaporate during the cooking, leaving a distinctly flavored bite. Makes 2½ cups.

¾ cup water
⅓ cup fresh lime juice
¼ cup gold tequila
2 tablespoons orange liqueur
2¼ cups sugar
½ teaspoon unsalted butter
3 tablespoons liquid pectin

Combine the water, lime juice, tequila, and liqueur in a large nonreactive saucepan. Add the sugar and butter. Bring the mixture to a full rolling boil. Quickly stir in the pectin. Return to a full rolling boil. Boil 1 minute, stirring constantly. Remove from the heat and skim off the foam with a metal spoon. Pour into a clean jar and let cool to room temperature. Cover and refrigerate. (The jelly may be stored in the refrigerator for up to 3 months.)

PRICKLY PEAR MARMALADE

After gathering cactus fruits in the desert (or in your specialty food shop), prepare this conserve, adapted from a recipe by Southwest wild foods expert Darcy Williamson. It is sensational. Makes about 5 cups.

2 oranges, thinly sliced
1 lemon, thinly sliced
1 pound ripe prickly pears, peeled, seeded, and chopped
2 tart green apples, peeled, cored, and chopped
1 package powdered pectin (1¾ to 2 ounces)
4 cups sugar
1 cup pine nuts

1] In a medium to large nonreactive saucepan, combine the oranges, lemon, and ½ cup water. Simmer until the rinds are tender, about 30 minutes. Remove from the heat and let stand, covered, overnight.

2] Add the prickly pears and apples. Bring the mixture to a full rolling boil to soften. Quickly stir in the pectin. Return to a full rolling boil. Add the sugar. Boil for 1 minute more, stirring constantly. The mixture will register 220°F on a candy thermometer. Remove from the heat and skim off the foam with a metal spoon. Add the pine nuts. Pour into clean jars and let cool to room temperature. Cover and refrigerate. (The jelly may be stored in the refrigerator for up to 3 months.)

RED CHILE HONEY

This flavored honey is very popular the Southwest. Use a desert honey, such as mesquite or saguaro if you can find it, or a mild local honey. Serve warmed to drizzle on sopaipillas or biscuits. Makes 2 cups.

¼ cup *caribe* (see page 137)
2 cups honey

Place the *caribe* in a small bowl and cover with boiling water. Let stand for 30 minutes to loosen the peel and soften. Strain and press the pulp to separate from the peel. In a medium saucepan, combine the chile pulp and honey. Bring to a simmer over low heat. Remove from the heat, pour into a pint jar, and let cool. Cover when completely cooled and store at room temperature. Let sit for 1 week before using, to allow flavors to meld.

PEACH HONEY

The Navajos were known for growing fabulous peaches, which once filled the Canyon de Chelly with their delicate perfume. Made with dried peach "ears," this flavored honey is easy to prepare. Makes about 2 cups.

½ pound dried peaches
1¼ cups mild honey, preferably saguaro, desert blossom, or sage honey

In a medium saucepan, combine the dried peaches and water to cover. Bring to a boil. Reduce the heat and simmer, uncovered, until the water is absorbed and fruit is soft, about 20 minutes. Remove from the heat and let cool completely. Puree in a food processor until smooth. With the motor running, pour in the honey. Transfer to a jar and cover. (The honey may be stored at room temperature for up to 1 week.)

OLD AND NEW SOUTHWEST INGREDIENTS

Following is a glossary of regional ingredients that are used in creating the traditional and contemporary flavors of Southwest-style breads in this recipe collection.

ACORNS

The smooth-shelled acorns gathered in July and August from Gambel and Emery oak trees can be eaten straight off the tree; they are indigenous to the Southwest. Other acorns need to be leached of their bitter tannin before roasting and grinding. Acorn meal is very nutty in flavor and deep brown in color. It is used extensively in Apache baking, especially for ash bread, a crusty flatbread baked in the coals of an open fire. Use acorn meal in a 50-50 combination with all-purpose, whole wheat, or graham flour in griddle breads, dumplings, biscuits, and yeast and quick breads. Or use like other whole nuts.
Making Acorn Meal: Shell the acorns like any other nut. Leach the acorns, if necessary, by placing shelled nuts in a clean cotton pillowcase or cheesecloth bag and submerging in running water, such as a clean stream or under a slow-running faucet, for up to 3 days. Knead the bag a few times each day to release the tannins. Dry in the sun. Toast the acorns, then grind in a food processor or nut mill into a meal.

AMARANTH

Amaranth *(Amaranthus hypochondriacus),* a grain about the size of a poppy seed, is high in calcium and phosphorus and contains approximately 16 percent protein and a high proportion of lysine, an essential amino acid rarely found in vegetable matter. Related to the common pigweed, amaranth has large seed heads; its spinachlike leaves and stems vary in color from purple to orange to white. Called the "Aztec grain" because of its use in early Mexican and Central American cultures for food as well as for religious ceremonies, it has a strong, wild flavor and a rather gelatinous texture. It is available as flour or a whole grain. Whole amaranth may be popped into tiny puffs, like popcorn. Adding the cooked grain to yeast and cornmeal batters helps baked goods to retain moisture and lightness.

BERRIES

Sweet local berries used by the various natives in breads include wolf berries, wild currants, elderberries, wild grapes, and desert hackberries. Chokeberries, too astringent to be eaten raw, make excellent syrups and preserves. Berries were often mashed fresh into ash cakes, dried like raisins for winter use and snacks, or dried and ground to add to quick breads (dried ground wild currants in corn bread was a favorite). Before the Spanish brought honey bees, berries were used as a primary sweetener.

BUTTERMILK

Buttermilk, *suero del la leche,* can be made from draining homemade butter or by culturing milk. It has a distinctive sour taste and is an unparalleled liquid addition to breads.

CANDIED AND SUNDRIED FRUITS AND VEGETABLES

Candied orange and grapefruit rinds, sweet potatoes, and pumpkin are added to pastries, breads, and savory picadillos. Sundried fruits include papaya, pineapple, pears, and apples. Tomatoes and chiles are favorite sundried vegetables.

CARIBE

Literally "crushed," *caribe* is any crushed dried chile, most often the small maroon New Mexican Chimayo chile, known for its hot sweet flavor.

CATTAIL FLOUR

A traditional desert flour—actually pollen—used by Pueblo bakers, cattail flour *(Typha augustifolia)* is used in combination with wheat flour in yeast and quick breads.
Making Cattail Flour: Strip the flowers from the upper part of the cattail stalks in summer when they are filled with pollen. Spread in a single layer on a baking sheet and toast at 350°F. until thoroughly dry, stirring every 10 minutes. Shake out and sieve the yellow pollen dust. (Store at room temperature in an airtight container.)

CHEESE

Making cheese *(queso),* was taught to the Indians by the Spanish. Early indigenous cheeses of the Southwest were made from goat's and ewe's milk. Use a mild French, stronger California, or New Mexican goat cheese or whole-milk ricotta to reproduce the tang of the soft-curd Southwest cheese. Feta or farmer cheese can be substituted for *queso fresco. Ranchero seca,* or ranch cheese, similar to farmer or cottage cheese, is still homemade in New Mexico and Texas from cow's, ewe's, or goat's milk. In the Southwest, Monterey jack is used as an all-purpose cheese; sharp Longhorn or Colby cheddar may be substituted. Mozzarella and string cheese are similar to the tangy white ball of *queso asadero* and the saltier *panela,* which are used for melting. Hard, aged grating cheeses, such as dry jack made from sheep's milk, and imported parmesan and romano, resemble the slightly dry, salty, sharp flavor of *queso cotija* and *queso anejo.* These cheeses are readily available in Hispanic as well as regular supermarkets. Check the freshness and quality of unfamiliar imported brands.

CHILES

Chiles are essential to all aspects of Southwest cuisine, including unusual savory breads and fillings. They range from mild to scalding hot; pungent to nonpungent; from yellow to bright green to deep red to chocolate brown; from smooth to rough to wrinkled; and from large, puffy rounds to slender oblongs to tiny finger-tip-size pellets. Chiles are available fresh, dried, crushed *(caribe),* and powdered *(molido).*

All cultivated varieties of chile grow green on the vine; as they ripen, they turn orange, red, or brown-red. Chiles are harvested and dried in the fall. In October and November the smell of roasting chiles fills the air as the big "squirrel cage" outdoor roasters set up along the roadsides char the pods. Climate and soil conditions as well as the variety contribute to the degree of hotness in a chile.

The most common large chiles are the New Mexico green chile (also known as Anaheim, California green chile, or chile verde) which turns red when ripe, and the dark green, thick-fleshed poblano which ranges from mild to a bit hot, depending on where it is grown (it is usually milder than the New Mexico green chiles). Red, yellow or purple bell peppers are also used extensively. The small fresh jalapeño and smoke-dried chipotle add rich flavor. Since there are so many different kinds of chiles, it is easy to become confused. They are not interchangeable in the recipes unless noted.
Roasting, Peeling, and Handling Fresh Chiles: Before roasting, either make a few incisions around the cap of the chile with a small paring knife to make sure that it doesn't explode, or cut it open and lay it flat. Wear rubber gloves or lightly oil your hands when handling chiles, and be sure to wash your hands with salt and strong soap after handling them. Remember not to touch your skin, especially around your eyes and mouth, until you've washed your hands.
Broiling or Grilling: Preheat the broiler and place the peppers on a baking sheet as close to the heat element

as possible. Using tongs, move peppers under the heat source until the skins are uniformly black. Peppers may also be grilled outdoors on a charcoal grill.

Stovetop: If you're using a gas stove, use the metal grid. Place a metal cake rack on the metal grid of the gas burner or over the electric burner. Turn the heat on high. Place the peppers directly in the flame. This is one of the fastest methods, since more surface is charred at once. Turn as necessary with tongs. Do not roast jalapeños, habaneros, or serranos in this manner, as they are too volatile.

Place the chiles in a heavy plastic bag and seal it airtight with a twist tie or rubber band. Allow the peppers to steam for at least 20 minutes or until cool enough to handle. Hold the peppers under cold running water and rub off the skin, peeling the outer skin downward. Remove inner ribs and seeds. Leave whole, if desired. Covered with plastic wrap, roasted and peeled peppers keep up to 3 days in the refrigerator. Whole roasted chiles may be frozen with the skin on. Defrost at room temperature and slip off the skins. Chiles may also be skinned and diced before freezing.

Toasting and Grinding Dried Chiles: Wipe the dried chiles with a soft, dry cloth if dusty. Place the chiles on an ungreased baking sheet. Toast in a 350°F. oven until the outer skin becomes plump and softens, 5 to 10 minutes, turning once. Toasting may also be done by shaking chiles in an ungreased heavy skillet or *comal* on the stovetop. Take care not to burn, crisp, or change their color. Cool completely. Break the chiles apart, discarding the stems, veins, and seeds of large chiles. Removing the seeds and veins of small chiles will diminish their hot edge. Crush chiles to flakes or grind to a powder of the desired consistency in a blender, food processor, or electric spice grinder. If using the traditional mortar and pestle, use extreme caution to protect your eyes from the airborne powder. (Store airtight in a cool, dry place.)

HOMEMADE CHILI POWDER
Makes about ⅓ cup

¼ cup red chile powder, mild, medium, hot,
    or a mixture to taste
1 tablespoon cumin seeds
1 teaspoon *each* ground coriander, garlic salt,
    and dried oregano
½ teaspoon *each* ground cloves and Hungarian paprika

1] Preheat the oven to 350°F.

2] Spread the chile powder on a baking sheet and toast for 3 to 4 minutes. Remove from the oven and let cool. Place the cumin seeds in a small skillet and toast over medium heat for 1 to 2 minutes, shaking the pan constantly to prevent burning. Let cool and grind to a fine powder in a spice grinder or blender.

3] Combine the chile powder, ground cumin, and all other spices and herbs in a small bowl. Mix until all ingredients are evenly combined. (Store in a tightly covered container in a cool, dry place.)

CHOCOLATE
Mexican chocolate reigns in the Southwest. It has a lower fat content than American or European semisweet chocolates. Ibarra and Mayordomo Mexican brands are marketed in tablets with almond and cinnamon flavors added. Mexican chocolate is often substituted for unsweetened chocolate in recipes. Alkalized Dutch process (also called European style) cocoa powder cannot be substituted.

MEXICAN HOT CHOCOLATE
Serves 2

    2 cups milk
    4 wedges sweet Mexican chocolate, chopped
        (about 2 ounces)

Heat the milk until just very hot, but not boiling, in a medium saucepan or in the microwave. Pour into an electric blender or use an immersion blender set into the saucepan. Add the chocolate and process until frothy and the chocolate is melted, about 15 seconds. Serve hot.

CORN
For information on corn, see pages 17–21.

CREMA MEXICANA
A very rich, thick, and tangy cultured cream available in Hispanic markets. If not available, substitute commercial sour cream or crème fraîche.

CREMA MEXICANA
Makes about 1 cup

    1 cup heavy (whipping) cream (not ultra-pasteurized)
    2 tablespoons buttermilk

In a small, nonreactive mixing bowl, combine the cream and buttermilk. Cover loosely with plastic wrap and let stand at room temperature until thickened, 8 to 24 hours. Stir to blend, cover, and refrigerate for up to 1 week.

FRUIT PASTE
Mango, guava, papaya, pineapple, and quince are often pureed and dried into blocks of fruit paste called *ate.* Small chunks of fruit paste are an excellent surprise center in muffins and sweet breads. (Fruit paste should be stored in the refrigerator after opening the package.) Serve as a spread by slicing in ⅛-inch-thick rectangles.

GOAT'S MILK
Goat's milk, or *leche de cabra,* is a traditional rural addition to breads; it may also be used as a one-for-one substitute for cow's milk. It is available fresh and as canned evaporated in grocery and health food stores.

HERBS AND SPICES
The most commonly used herbs are wild marjoram, Mexican oregano, *tuitsma* (chinchweed), and white sage. Mexican mint marigold *(yerbanis)* is similar to tarragon. Rosemary is also widely used. Imported saffron is expensive, but *azafrán,* or safflower, is an inexpensive alternative; use double the amount in recipes calling for saffron. Cooling leaves of fresh cilantro and *yerba buena,* a spearmint, often wild, complement fiery chiles. Herbs and leaves may be toasted before use on a *comal* to bring out their flavor. Flower blossoms, such as hibiscus and chamomile are also prevalent, and may be served with homebaked breads. Cumin is a predominant Southwest flavor in some chili powders. The licorice-flavored anise, cinnamon, ginger, and coriander seeds are also popular, especially in pastries and sweet breads. Cinnamon stick is best ground fresh in a spice or coffee grinder.

HONEY
Honey is a popular ingredient in Southwest cooking. Wild brush, clover, sage blossom, desert blossom, and local cactus honeys, such as the mild saguaro, pitchy mesquite, aromatic palo verde, and assertive prickly pear, are favorites. Red Chile Honey (page 135) is popular around Taos and may be used as a topping for or ingredient in breads.

Lard

Lard, *manteca,* is clarified pork fat, white and solid, a flavorful traditional ingredient in the rustic Indian and pioneer breads of the Southwest. It is also melted for deep-frying Indian fry breads. Surprisingly lower in fat and cholesterol than butter, it is best homemade. Solid vegetable shortening, butter, margarine, or chicken fat may be substituted one-for-one for lard in bread recipes.

Rendering Lard: Buy lard from a butcher shop or good meat counter. Cut a 1- to 2-pound piece of leaf lard into small pieces and place in a deep heavy roasting pan. Place in a preheated 300°F. oven to render or cook down to form a clear liquid. As the lard starts to render, pour the liquid into a bowl to cool. As more liquid forms, pour it into the bowl. It will set up creamy and white. When all of the lard is rendered, the cracklings will remain. They can be used in place of bacon in corn bread recipes. (Homemade lard may be stored in the refrigerator for up to 4 months.)

Mesquite Flour

The mesquite tree provided shelter, weapons, fuel, and a high-protein food. The fruity tasting flour can be substituted for cornmeal in bread, muffin, and pancake recipes; some wheat flour is needed for texture.

Making Mesquite Flour: Spread mesquite pods on baking sheets and toast in an oven on the lowest setting until thoroughly dried and crisp, 1 to 3 hours. Grind immediately in small batches in a blender or food processor. Sift through a sieve to remove the fiber and seeds.

Oil

Although olive oil was used in many traditional recipes, it was usually too expensive for daily use in the colonial Southwest. Cold-pressed corn, canola, and sunflower seed oils may also be used.

Panocha Flour

Panocha flour, *harina enraizada,* is made from sprouted wheat berries. It is sweeter in taste and rougher in texture than regular whole wheat flour. It is traditionally used during Lent for panocha pudding, the Mexican dessert. In Mexican groceries, *piloncillo* (see page 141) is often called *panocha.* Panocha flour can also be made from sprouted oat groats.

Making Panocha Flour: Soak wheat berries overnight in a bowl at room temperature. Wash and drain through a double layer of cheesecloth. Lay the cheesecloth on a flat plate and spread out the soaked berries. Cover with plastic wrap or slip into a large plastic bag to retain the moisture. Leave at room temperature until just sprouted, 2 to 3 days. Spread out to dry at room temperature on a clean baking sheet. When dry, grind in a food processor to a coarse flour. Use immediately.

Pepitas

Pepitas are raw hulled pumpkin seeds; they vary in size from tiny to over an inch long. *Pepitas* may be used toasted whole or ground. They are also used to make a sweet nut paste filling for pastries. Other winter squash and melon seeds are dried and used in the same manner.

Toasting Pepitas: Toss raw hulled pumpkin seeds with oil to coat evenly (use 1 tablespoon vegetable oil for every ½ cup *pepitas).* Spread the seeds out on a baking sheet lined with parchment paper or aluminum foil. Bake in the center of a preheated 300°F. oven until crisp and golden, 15 to 20 minutes, stirring occasionally. Let cool before using. Store in an airtight container at room temperature up to 2 weeks.

PILONCILLO

An unrefined sugar produced in rustic sugar mills in Mexico, *piloncillo* is shaped into small, hard cones. The deeper the color, the stronger the flavor. Packed light or dark brown sugar may be substituted: One cone equals ½ cup. (Purists use dark brown sugar and add a tablespoon of molasses per each cone to reproduce the flavor more exactly, but this is optional.) (*Piloncillo* should be stored in an airtight container at room temperature.)
Using Piloncillo: Soften in a microwave oven for 1 to 2 minutes, then grate on a small hand grater or grind in a food processor.

PIÑON

Piñon (pine nuts) are the seeds of a large Spanish scrub pine tree, *Pinus edulis,* the New Mexico state tree. The Navajo were known to use every part of the tree for building, for medicine, dyes, and baskets, as well as food. The nuts are still gathered by hand. Shelled pine nuts are generally available, mainly imported from Asia and Europe. To restore nuts which have lost their crispness, toast at 200°F. for 10 to 15 minutes. When toasted, the unique rich nut flavor is mellowed. Piñons are a splendid addition to breads of all kinds. (Piñons may be stored in an airtight container in the freezer for up to 1 year.)

PISTACHIO NUTS

Alamogordo pistachios, legendary in New Mexico, tolerate extreme temperatures and are low in saturated fat. The primary grower is Eagle Ranch in Alamogordo with their "Heart of the Desert" nuts, which were planted only in 1974. For ½ cup nutmeats, shell 1 cup nuts. (Pistachio nuts may be stored in an airtight container in the freezer for up to 1 year.)
Blanching Pistachio Nuts: Put the nuts in a heatproof bowl and pour boiling water to cover them. Let nuts stand for 1 minute. Drain and turn the nuts out onto a dish towel and rub off the skins. Dry on a baking sheet in a 300°F. oven for 10 minutes.

PRICKLY PEARS

Prickly pears grow on a treelike cactus related to the saguoro. It is found throughout the Southwest. The edible pads, *nopalitos,* and red fruit, *tunas,* ripen in August and September. The stickers are so sharp that it's advisable to use tongs to remove the pears from the plant. Prickly pears make excellent jams and jellies (see page 135). They go well with vanilla, dates, brandy, and honey and make a wonderful fruit sauce for pancakes and waffles when sweetened and thickened with a bit of cornstarch. The peeled fruit can be mashed and used as a substitute for applesauce in bread recipes.
Peeling Prickly Pears: Holding the fruit with tongs, use a vegetable brush to scrub off the stickers under running water. Blanch for 15 seconds in boiling water. Wearing rubber gloves, immediately slip off the skins.

PUMPKIN

Pumpkins are just one of hundreds of varieties of winter squash, or *calabaza,* which is characterized by a hard outer shell and an interior that turns smooth when cooked. They range in size from small and ribbed to large as a watermelon and may be baked, braised, or boiled. The seeds, known as *pepitas* (see page 140), are dried and toasted. Winter squashes have been grown since the Anasazi and Hohokam cultures of the Southwest. An early method of preservation was to roast winter squashes, slice them, and then sun-dry them for rehydration later. Winter squash and pumpkin may be used interchangeably. Pumpkin or winter squash puree is an excellent addition to breads.
Pureeing Fresh Pumpkin or Winter Squash: Wash the whole pumpkin or winter squash and cut off the top. Some small winter squashes may be cooked whole, but others have to be cut in half. Scrape out seeds and spongy fibers. Cut into large cubes, leaving the skin on. Place in a baking dish, flesh side down, with a little water. Cover and bake at 350°F. for 1 to 1½ hours, or until the flesh is tender when pierced with a knife. Drain, cool, then peel off and discard the skin. Puree the pulp until smooth in a blender, food

mill, or food processor. Cool, cover, then refrigerate or freeze. About 1 pound of raw pumpkin or winter squash will yield about 1 cup cooked puree.

Quinoa

Quinoa, a very ancient crop once cultivated in the Andes, is now successfully grown commercially in Colorado. Quinoa has the highest protein content of any grain (about 17 percent), which is why it is sometimes called the "super grain." Best grown at altitudes above 10,000 feet, it positively flourishes under extreme conditions including thin air, hot sun, frost, and drought. Quinoa must be thoroughly rinsed before it can be used. Because it is coated with saponin, a resin-like substance with a bitter, soapy taste that repels insects, rinse and drain the quinoa about 5 times with cold running water until the water runs clear. Quinoa is a member of the pigweed family *(chenopodium),* a staple in Native kitchens. It is available as flour or a whole grain.

Saguaro Fruit

Saguaro fruit looks like a miniature spiked watermelon; it has an inedible green rind and red inner flesh dotted with tiny black seeds. The fruit is harvested in mid-July. Saguaro puree may be used like applesauce in quick breads or made into jelly.
Pureeing Saguaro Fruit: Slit the rind with a small knife and loosen the pulp with your thumbs. Puree in a food processor until smooth. Use right away. (Saguaro puree may be frozen for up to 6 months.

Shortening

Solid vegetable shortening is a flavorless white fat made from purified vegetable oil processed under heat with hydrogen. It is 100 percent fat, and it is high in saturated fat since it contains palm oil. It is often used in making tortillas and breads or heated for cooking fry breads. It is an ideal substitute for lard.

Summer Squash

Native to the Southwest, summer squash, was of ceremonial importance to the Southwest Indians, and it was a food crop for the Spanish. Green zucchini and yellow summer squash are excellent grated raw into bread doughs, adding moisture, color, and texture.

Sunflower Seeds

The sunflower *(Helianthus annus)* was domesticated before corn in the Southwest. The seeds were beaten off the ripe flower heads in the fall. After winnowing, parching, and grinding the seeds on the metate, the meal was used in ash cakes and an atole drink (see page 20). Today the seeds are eaten raw or roasted.

Tepary Beans

Dried tepary beans, both wild and cultivated, have been ground into flour by the desert peoples of the Southwest and northern Mexico since about 3000 B.C. It is used especially by the Tohono O'odham of Arizona, hence their name, the Bean People. Use a small amount of ground beans in tortillas, fry breads, and quick breads. Tepary beans are available in health food stores and by mail order.
Grinding Tepary Beans: Grind the dried beans by hand with a *mano* and *metate,* or in a hand or electric grain mill. Best combined with corn or wheat flours.

Tequila

Distilled blue agave cactus juice from Mexico, tequila is a popular spirit for cooking with a strong, herbal flavor. It is used in Margarita Jelly (page 134).

Tomatoes

Tomatoes are an integral part of Southwest baking, either as a puree, sun-dried bits, or part of a savory filling.

Vanilla

Vanilla, a highly fragrant member of the orchid family, is native to the New World. The Spanish word, *vainilla,* meaning little pod, refers to the long slender pod that contains the seeds. The Indians developed the technique of making extract by picking the pods before they ripen and removing the crystals from outside the pods. Vanilla is used to flavor a variety of sweet breads and drinks. Use vanilla beans, pure vanilla extract, or vanilla sugar, not imitation vanilla.

Making Homemade Vanilla Extract: Submerge 2 whole vanilla beans in a pint of good brandy. Let stand for about 2 weeks. (The vanilla extract may be stored indefinitely, tightly covered in a cool dark place.)

Hot Vanilla Breakfast Drink
Serves 2

> 1 cup milk
> ¼ cup heavy (whipping) cream
> ⅔ vanilla bean
> 1 tablespoon honey or sugar, or to taste
> Ground cinnamon, preferably freshly ground, to taste

Combine the milk, heavy cream, and vanilla bean in a small saucepan. Heat to scalding. Remove from the heat and let steep 20 minutes. Rewarm and whisk the mixture. Remove the vanilla bean, split it, and scrape out the seeds into the warm milk. Add honey or sugar and sprinkle with cinnamon. Serve hot.

Wheat

High-gluten hard red winter wheat is grown in Texas and Colorado, with Deaf Smith County organic wheat sold nationally through Arrowhead Mills. Some of the best durum wheat, good for bread and pasta, is grown in the Southwest breadbasket around Tucson and Yuma. Wheat was brought to the Southwest by the Spanish from Sonora. The Indians immediately adopted the grain for making breads. Look for *harina de trigo* (whole wheat flour) and *harina blanco* (bleached white flour) sold in ten-pound cotton sacks in supermarkets and Hispanic markets. Use unbleached all-purpose or bread flour for best results in making homemade bread.

Wild Wheat

Commercially cultivated and trademarked in English as WildWheat by ecologists Nick and Susana Yensen, this high-protein grain *(Distichlis palmeri)* is a member of the halophyte seed family of salt- and temperature-tolerant cereal plants indigenous to the southern Arizona desert. Known as *trigo gentil* in Spanish, it was grown by the Cocopah Indians at the mouth of the Colorado River, where it was watered by salty tidal waters from the Gulf of California up until the eighteenth century. It tastes and feels just like regular whole wheat flour but contains very low gluten. Use as a substitute for other glutenless flours with regular wheat flour or as a direct substitute for wheat in yeast and quick breads. Due to low yields, it is rarely seen for sale, and then for exorbitant prices. It is sometimes included in multi-grain flour mixes.

Yeast

Today's leavened breads are created by a one-celled natural living microorganism called yeast. To be activated and multiply, yeast needs the combination of sugar, moisture, warmth, and air. Yeast produces a stretchy meshlike gluten structure in a dough. The heat of the oven kills the yeast, burns off the alcohol by-product of the expanding carbon dioxide, and sets the porous pattern and familiar texture of bread. Yeast is killed by too much heat, 140°F. or above; below 50°F., it goes into a suspended state, allowing dough to be refrigerated or frozen for periods of time. Maximum rising occurs between 80° and 90°F.

Yeast is sold to the consumer in many different forms. As with all culinary choices, let availability, your palate, and the taste of the final product guide you to which yeast to use.

Active dry yeast is sold in dated ¼-ounce foil-wrapped flat packets, in 4-ounce jars, or in bulk. One scant tablespoon of dry yeast is equal to a ¼-ounce package or a .06-ounce cube of fresh cake yeast. I generally use 1 to 1½ teaspoons dry yeast to 3 cups white flour, with whole-grain flours needing a bit more. Dry yeast is not activated until dissolved in a warm liquid (about 105° to 115°F.). It is advisable to invest in a good yeast or candy thermometer to be certain of the liquid temperatures until you can recognize the exact warmth by feel. Without a thermometer, test by dripping a few drops on the inside of your wrist. It should feel warm without being uncomfortably hot, as for baby formula. If the liquid is too cool, the yeast will be slow to activate. If it is too hot, the yeast may be killed, in which case it will fail to produce the characteristic foamy effect, and the dough will not rise. (Active dry yeast should be stored in a tightly covered container in the refrigerator.)

Compressed fresh cake yeast can be used interchangeably with active dry yeast, which I have used throughout this book. It is sold in .06-ounce and 2-ounce cakes and 1-pound blocks, sometimes available from your local bakery. Fresh yeast is highly perishable: it must be refrigerated and will keep for only about 2 weeks. When fresh, it is an even tan-gray with no discoloration and breaks with a clean edge. Compressed yeast needs to be dissolved in lukewarm liquids (about 95°F.) before being added to the dry ingredients.

Fast-rising or quick-rising yeasts were developed to shorten rising times. You can substitute this type of yeast for regular active dry, but I find slower rising breads have the better flavor and texture.

TRADITIONAL EQUIPMENT AND SPECIAL BAKING UTENSILS

The following is a list of the most important new and antique hand tools and bakeware mentioned in this book to create traditional-style Southwest breads. Of course you will also have miscellaneous tools such as liquid and dry measuring cups, hand graters, stainless steel and glass mixing bowls, plastic storage containers, pastry brushes, wire whisks, large plastic spatulas, metal and plastic scrapers, a serrated knife, and wooden and metal kitchen spoons close at hand. A food processor and a heavy-duty electric mixer (I use a KitchenAid) for heavy doughs are essential tools in my bake kitchen.

BREAD PANS

Every bread dough is formed into either a freeform or a molded loaf. Traditional Southwest Indian and Spanish breads are usually hand-formed and baked without a mold or in layer cake pans. Loaf pans are used to give form to loaves that may not be strong enough to hold their own shape. Different sizes and shapes of pans give breads and muffins their individual character. Standard loaf pans come in the 9-by-5-by-3-inch size, 8½-by-4½-inches, and 7-by-3 inches; smaller sizes are also handy, included linked mini loaf pans. Department, hardware, and specialty stores offer an astonishing choice of pans, both in size and material.

Baking pans come in many different kinds of materials, each with its own qualities. Consider which pans work best in your oven to produce the type of loaf you like best. No matter what size pan is used, formed dough should fill to half or two-thirds the pan: less, and you will have a flat loaf; more, an overflowing top-heavy loaf that looks awkward and is difficult to slice. Small loaf pans are often welded together in a "strap" or linked form for easy handling. If you tend to bake multiple loaves, investigate restaurant supply stores which carry straps in various sizes. If you are using small individual pans, place them on a baking sheet during the rising and baking to eliminate a lot of awkward juggling.

In addition to loaf pans, square and rectangular pans, baking sheets, and sheet pans are used for the breads in this book. Look for well-constructed pans of heaviest-gauge aluminum or tin-plated steel. Black steel is fine, but be aware that the finish causes a dark, heavy crust. Baking sheets are also available in air-cushioned and nonstick types. When baking at high oven temperatures, stack 2 baking sheets together ("double panning") to slow the temperature and prevent the bottoms of the baked goods from burning.

The Anglo pioneer's all-purpose baking pan was the cast-iron skillet, from 6 to 18 inches in diameter. Dutch ovens were used for fry breads and for outdoor baking. Heat diffuses evenly through cast iron, but it is slow to heat up and cool down. Always wear very heavy oven mitts to prevent burns when handling this type of cookware. Old recipes call for lining cast-iron pans with oiled heavy brown paper or corn husks or sprinkling them with cornmeal to prevent sticking, but seasoned pans don't need this precaution. If you plan to use antique cast iron equipment, be certain to have it thoroughly cleaned before seasoning. *Seasoning Cast-Iron:* Scrub the pan with liquid detergent and hot water, rinse thoroughly, and dry. Apply a coating of vegetable oil, shortening, or Pam spray shortening onto all of the interior surfaces. Place the pan over medium-low heat for 30 minutes, until smoking, taking care not to let the oil burn. Using heavy mitts, remove from the heat and let cool. Repeat the process three to four times, as needed. Reseason if the pan becomes rusty or discolored. Maintain the protective coating by wiping out with a damp cloth (never use a scouring pad) and drying well. Regrease when necessary by applying a light layer of Pam spray shortening. The buildup of layers of grease "sweeten" the iron and prevent sticking.

COMALS

A *comal* is a flat round cast-iron or steel griddle, 12 to 30 inches in diameter, specifically designed for baking and reheating tortillas to a high temperature over an open fire. It needs to be well-seasoned and never washed with water to prevent rusting. To clean, scrape off any cooking residue with a metal spatula, rinse under hot water, and dry immediately with paper towels. A *comal* may also be made in the traditional way of heavy unglazed earthenware pottery; these should be seasoned like other clay cookware.

CLAY BAKEWARE

Mexican earthenware *cazuela* pottery for cooking, as well as tableware, is world famous for its beauty as well as its functionalism. Earthenware was used exclusively for many centuries for baking, broiling, and stovetop direct heat cooking. The *olla* is the traditional deep pot for cooking beans. New pottery must be of good quality, as there can be a high lead content in poorly glazed earthenware. Unglazed pottery presents no problem. New pottery must be sealed before use.

Sealing Clay Cookware: Rub the outside of the container with a clove of raw garlic. Fill with soapy water to the rim. Bring to a boil and continue to simmer at a low boil until all the water has evaporated. Remove immediately and carefully from the heat and let stand until cooled.

Clay loaf pans give a crust similar to loaves baked in a *horno.* They come in the 8½-by-4½-inch loaf pan size. Whether glazed or unglazed on the inside, these pans are heavy and are slow, steady conductors of heat. Always place clay pans on the lowest oven rack for the bottom of the bread to brown properly. Avoid sugary doughs, which will stick to the porous clay. Generally, it takes 10 minutes longer to bake a loaf in a clay pan than in a metal pan. Scrub with soap and water to clean, and dry completely before storing.

Seasoning Clay Loaf Pans: Clay loaf pans need to be seasoned only before using the first time. Scrub the cookware with liquid detergent and hot water and rinse thoroughly. Spread a light coating of vegetable oil or Pam spray shortening inside the pan and wipe out the excess with a paper towel. Place the cookware in a 250°F. oven for 1 hour. Remove from the oven and place on a thick pot holder or wire rack to cool.

LA CLOCHE

La Cloche is the trademarked name for an unglazed ceramic oven baker. It is used to recreate the hot steaminess of a stone oven to produce thin, crisp crusts.

Using La Cloche: Form the dough into a round loaf a bit smaller than the bottom dish. Spray the bottom with a cooking spray and sprinkle with flour or cornmeal. Place the dough ball in the center. Dust the top with more flour. Cover with a clean towel and let rest at room temperature about 30 minutes, or until double in bulk. Meanwhile, fill the cover with tap water in the kitchen sink or bathtub. Preheat the oven to 425°F. Decoratively slash the surface of the loaf as desired. Drain the bell cover, leaving it dripping wet, and cover the bread. Place the La Cloche in the center of the preheated oven. Remove the cover after 30 minutes of baking to allow the loaf to brown thoroughly. Reduce the oven temperature to 400°F. and continue to bake for another 15 to 20 minutes, or until golden brown and hollow sounding. Carefully remove the baker from the oven with thick oven mitts, and remove the loaf to a rack to cool. To clean the dish, tap out the excess flour and scrub off any stuck-on bits with a brush and water only, as soap can impart a taste into the next baked loaf.

MANO Y METATE

The rustic stone *mano* and *metate* are the age-old Native household tools for grinding corn into meal. The *metate,* a heavy flat oval mortar with low sides, sits flat on the floor, and the *mano,* a smooth tapered grinding stone, is handheld. Grinding stones for corn vary in roughness to produce coarse to medium meals and fine flours. The stones are cured with spruce gum and blessed prior to use by a designated holy man. They are lifetime possessions. Modern bakers grind corn with a meat grinder set on successively smaller grinds, or they use a traditional hand corn mill. *Tempering a new metate or molcajete:* Sprinkle the *metate* with ¼ to ½ cup raw rice mixed with 1 tablespoon of salt. Grind repeatedly, rinse the rice, and return it to the *metate*. Repeat about half a dozen times until the ground grain is clean colored and free of small pieces of rocks. Whole roasted corn kernels are easiest to grind when warmed for 10 minutes in a 350°F. oven. Hand or electric grain mills, and food processors are a convenient alternative. Clean stone grinders by scrubbing with a heavy brush and clear water, as soap will leave a distinct taste.

MOLCAJETE Y TEJOLOTE

A *molcajete,* a three-legged black basalt rock or granite mortar, and *tejolote,* or pestle, are traditionally used for hand-grinding in the Southwest kitchen. The *tejolote* should be about 3 inches long and 2 inches wide for best results. They are especially useful for grinding toasted cumin seeds, fresh red chile powders, cacoa pods, salsas, and fresh chile pastes. Often a fresh salsa is brought to the table in its *molcajete.* The two are also sometimes referred to as *liquedore azteca,* or Indian blender. A coffee grinder or small electric mill can be used for grinding spice powders and a food mill with the coarse blade or blender or food processor for pureeing. The *molcajete* is easily confused with the *metate,* the stone basin used for grinding corn.

PARCHMENT PAPER

Parchment paper is a nonporous, silicone-treated heat- and grease-resistant paper. I use it to line pans when making hand-fashioned loaves instead of greasing them. Parchment paper is available in rolls or sheets in most supermarkets and cookware shops. Do not substitute wax paper, which will burn, or brown paper grocery bags, which are made from recycled paper, with inedible chemicals mixed into the pulp.

ROLLING PIN

A small rolling pin, sometimes called a tortilla roller or palote (literally, wood stick in Spanish), 7 inches long and 2 inches in diameter, is used for rolling out fry breads and slap breads. A thin wood French rolling pin or small American ball-bearing pin are good substitutes, as larger pastry rolling pins can put too much pressure on the delicate doughs. A clean and sanded sawed-off broom handle can also be used. A Mexican rolling pin is also referred to as a *bollito* or *rodillo.*

STIR STICKS

Stir sticks, called *ádístsiin* in the Navajo kitchen, also prevalent in Pueblo kitchens, made from native Southwest greasewood, are used for stirring cornmeal mush, which can be the basis for breads such as Taos Sun Bread (page 46), dumplings, and finger breads. They range from a long, thick stick the size of a broom handle to four thin ones, less than half an inch in diameter, tied together for whisking. Wooden spoons and wire whisks are modern substitutes.

TORTILLA PRESS

A tortilla press made of wood, aluminum, or heavy cast metal is used to flatten corn or empanada doughs, which can be difficult to roll out evenly by hand. It is not necessary for flour tortillas; they are easier to roll out due to the gluten. The 6- to 6½-inch diameter press is preferred by most cooks. When using a hand press, place the tortilla between layers of plastic wrap to protect the delicate dough from contact with the metal. Antique or new wooden models made from mesquite wood are sometimes available. An electric press presses and bakes the tortilla in one step.

OLD AND NEW SOUTHWEST RESOURCES

Many special food products are used in this recipe book to prepare breads with a characteristic Southwest flavor.
Although most of the ingredients are available in ordinary supermarkets, Hispanic markets, and natural foods stores throughout the
United States, included here is a list of reliable mail-order sources for regional ingredients as well as special cooking equipment.
Many of the very small companies do not take phone orders; they send you their catalog and you order by mail.
The Santa Fe School of Cooking, along with the Coyote General Store and the Old Southwest Trading Company,
is an excellent one-stop shopping resource since it carries standard and hard-to-find products.

ARROWHEAD MILLS, INC.
BOX 2059
HEREFORD, TX 79045-2059
800-749-0730
Fine-grind blue cornmeal, quinoa,
amaranth, teff, and chick pea flour;
hearty organic grains

❋

COYOTE CAFÉ GENERAL STORE
132 W. WATER STREET
SANTA FE, NM 87501
800-866-HOWL
Fine-grind blue cornmeal, quinoa,
amaranth, teff, and chick pea flour;
hearty organic grains

❋

DESERT GROVE, INC.
P.O. BOX DRAWER B
LAS CRUCES, NM 88004-1898
800-654-6887
Pecans

EAGLE RANCH PISTACHIO GROVES
RT. 1 BOX 257
ALAMOGORDO, NM 88310
800-432-0999
Pistachios

❋

EARTHSTONE WOOD-FIRE OVENS
1233 NO. HIGHLAND AVENUE
LOS ANGELES, CA 90038
213-656-5926
Anglo-style indoor and outdoor
wood-fire ovens

❋

FREIDA'S, INC.
4465 CORPORATE CENTER DRIVE
LOS ALAMITOS, CA 90720
714-826-6100
Colorado-grown fine-grind red and
Hopi blue cornmeals

LOS CHILEROS
P.O. BOX 6215
SANTA FE, NM 87501
505-471-6967
Blue corn products, dried chiles

❋

MOZZARELLA CHEESE CO.
2944 ELM STREET
DALLAS, TX 75226
214-741-4072
Fresh cheeses with Italian and Southwest
flavors

❋

NATIVE SEED/SEARCH
2509 N. CAMPBELL AVENUE #325
TUCSON, AZ 85719
520-327-9123
Native seed bank, blue cornmeals,
many-colored posole (hominy), winter
squash seeds, amaranth and mesquite
flour, publications

OLD SOUTHWEST TRADING COMPANY
P.O. BOX 7545
ALBUQUERQUE, NM 87194
505-836-0168
Blue corn products, dried chiles

✳

OVEN CRAFTERS
BOX 24
TOMALES, CA 94971
415-663-9010
Plans for backyard Southwest-style bread ovens

✳

QUINOA CORPORATION
2300 CENTRAL AVENUE, STE. G
BOULDER, CO 80301
800-237-2304
Whole quinoa and flour

✳

RANCH O CASADO
P.O. BOX 1149
SAN JUAN PUEBLO, NM 87566
505-852-4482
Cornmeal and posole *(hominy) from local pueblo corn*

✳

SANTA FE SCHOOL OF COOKING
116 W. SAN FRANCISCO STREET
SANTA FE, NM 87501
505-983-4511
Excellent stone-ground cornmeals, equipment

✳

SEEDS OF CHANGE
1364 RUFINA CIRCLE #5
SANTA FE, NM 87501
505-438-8080
Heirloom grain seeds

✳

WINTER SUN TRADING CO.
18 EAST SANTA FE AVENUE
FLAGSTAFF, AZ 86001
602-774-2884
Culinary ash, azafrán, *herbs, and spices*

✳

TABLE OF CONVERSIONS

The exact equivalents in the following tables have been rounded for convenience.

US/UK
oz=ounce
lb=pound
in=inch
ft=foot
tbl=tablespoon
fl oz=fluid ounce
qt=quart

METRIC
g=gram
kg=kilogram
mm=millimeter
cm=centimeter
ml=milliliter
l=liter

WEIGHTS

US/UK	Metric
1 oz	28 g
2 oz	56 g
3 oz	84 g
4 oz (¼ lb)	112 g
5 oz (⅓ lb)	140 g
6 oz	168 g
7 oz	196 g
8 oz (½ lb)	224 g
10 oz	280 g
12 oz (¾ lb)	296 g
14 oz	392 g
16 oz (1 lb)	450 g
1½ lb	675 g
2 lb	900 g
3 lb	1350 g

LENGTH MEASURES

⅛ in	3 mm
¼ in	6 mm
½ in	12 mm
1 in	2.5 cm
2 in	5 cm
3 in	7.5 cm
4 in	10 cm
5 in	13 cm
6 in	15 cm
7 in	18 cm
8 in	20 cm
9 in	23 cm
10 in	25 cm
11 in	28 cm
12/1 ft	30 cm

OVEN TEMPERATURES

Fahrenheit	Celsius	Gas
250	120	½
275	140	1
300	150	2
325	160	3
350	180	4
375	190	5
400	200	6
425	220	7
450	230	8
475	240	9
500	260	10

LIQUIDS

US	Metric	UK
2 tbl	30 ml	1 fl oz
¼ cup	60 ml	2 fl oz
⅓ cup	80 ml	3 fl oz
½ cup	125 ml	4 fl oz
⅔ cup	160 ml	5 fl oz
¾ cup	180 ml	6 fl oz
1 cup	250 ml	8 fl oz
1½ cups	375 ml	12 fl oz
2 cups	500 ml	16 fl oz
4 cups/1 qt	1 l	32 fl oz

HIGH ALTITUDE GUIDE

Because there is less atmospheric pressure at high altitudes,
carbon dioxide expands quicker and baking adjustments are needed to control leavening power.
Yeast and quick breads both rise faster at high altitudes, baking up very coarse grained.

YEAST

Starting at 3,000 feet, reduce yeast by ½ teaspoon for every tablespoon or package of yeast listed in the recipe. Let the dough rise until it is barely double in volume to avoid overrising. Many bakers deflate the dough several times instead of once or add eggs to develop a finer texture.

BAKING SODA AND BAKING POWDER

For each teaspoon, decrease by ⅛ teaspoon at more than 3,000 feet; ¼ teaspoon at more than 5,000 feet. In quick breads, use only three-quarters of the specified amount called for in the recipe, taking care not to add less than ½ teaspoon of baking soda per cup of sour liquid to neutralize the acid.

LIQUIDS

For each cup, increase the amount by 1 tablespoon at more than 3,000 feet; 2 to 3 tablespoons at 5,000 feet; and 3 to 4 tablespoons at 7,000 to 8,000 feet.

SUGAR

For each cup, decrease the amount by 1 tablespoon at more than 3,000 feet; 2 tablespoons at 5,000 feet; and 3 tablespoons at 7,000 to 8,000 feet.

FLOUR

For each cup, increase the amount by 1 tablespoon at more than 3,000 feet; 2 tablespoons at 5,000 feet; and 3 tablespoons at more than 6,500 feet.

DEEP-FRY

Lower the temperature of the oil by 3°F. for every 1,000 feet above 3,000 feet.

INDEX

Laurie Smith wishes to extend her thanks to
Kathi Long for her beautiful baking, to Jody Apple for the use of her enchanting bed and breakfast,
Rancho Manzana, in Chimayo, New Mexico, as a backdrop for the bread, to Molly Polk for her energy
and enthusiasm as an assistant, to Joe Evans for his invitation to participate in an afternoon of adobe oven baking,
to Deborah Madison and Jane Stacy for their heartfelt guidance, to Yolanda Calzadiaz for her tortillas,
to Crucita Romero for her oven bread, and especially to Bobby and Jamie
for their unending patience, support and love.